TORN ASUNDER

WORKBOOK

TORN ASUNDER

WORKBOOK

DAVE CARDER

MOODY PUBLISHERS

CHICAGO

© 2001, 2008

DAVID M. CARDER

All Web sites listed herein are accurate at the time of publication, but may change in the future or cease to exist. The listing of Web site references and resources does not imply publisher endorsement of the site's entire contents. Groups, corporations, and organizations are listed for informational purposes, and listing does not imply publisher endorsement of their activities.

Second Edition Editor: Christopher Reese
Cover Design: Garborg Design Works
Cover Image: iStockphoto
Interior Design: Smartt Guys design

ISBN: 978-0-8024-7136-9

We hope you enjoy this book from Moody Publishers. Our goal is to provide high-quality, thought-provoking books and products that connect truth to your real needs and challenges. For more information on other books and products written and produced from a biblical perspective, go to www.moodypublishers.com or write to:

Moody Publishers
820 N. LaSalle Boulevard
Chicago, IL 60610

5 7 9 10 8 6 4

Printed in the United States of America

CONTENTS

Introduction: A Time for Growth

Infidelity is much like a wildfire that destroys a preserve and all living things in it. But a wildfire also burns away the debris and the underbrush choking the forest's new growth. Though infidelity initially devastates a relationship, a marriage can not only recover from adultery, but flourish after it. The process takes time, a safe environment, appropriate nurture, lots of patience, and God's grace. It is a time of vital personal growth for both spouses.

This workbook will start you on that journey. It is a map that shows you the lay of the land. It will be your survival guide for the next one hundred days. You won't be finished with this wildfire, but you will have it contained by then. You will be "mopping up" and putting out "hot spots" over the next several months. But best of all during that time, you will be replanting new growth personally and relationally.

You are probably in the thick of the wildfire now. You need to be tough-minded to stay there and fight it out. It will always be easier to run to what looks like safety. But just like it's easier to fight fire with a partner, so it is true of fighting infidelity. Two spouses need to be involved in this process. At times you might need to call in additional support, such as a pastor, a therapist, or close friends. If the infidelity is complicated with disease, pregnancy, career ruination, or lawsuits, you most assuredly will need professional help. And at times, you may need to take some breaks—take them. Don't wear yourself out trying to be too strong. Lean on your network of supports such as family, friends, coworkers, and small groups. Each of you will need all the help you can get.

DEFINITIONS AND PURPOSES

Before we get started, though, we need to look at some definitions and purposes in this workbook.

Consistent with the original book, the *Torn Asunder Workbook* uses the following terms to identify the various characters:

Infidel: The spouse who committed the infidelity.
Partner: The individual with whom the infidel was involved.
Spouse: The spouse who has been faithful.

As you seek to recover from a marital affair, this workbook will guide you toward five outcomes. It will:

1. Stabilize the marriage in the initial crisis.
2. Provide structure for this emotionally volatile environment.
3. Bring closure to the "old" marriage—the marriage prior to the affair.
4. Set established skills necessary for the "new" marriage pattern.
5. Answer the questions: How could you do this to me? Why did you do it?

Overview of the Process

Much of the first half of this workbook will be spent looking back at the affair: understanding the dynamics that fed into it, identifying the marital pattern and the circumstances and interpersonal relationships that finally reached "critical mass" where an affair became inevitable.

Each of you individually will work on your contribution to the deterioration of the marriage. Each of you will work on a forgiveness letter specific to your contributions. You will read that letter to each other, and the infidel will also prepare an affair forgiveness letter. Throughout this initial process, your homework will focus upon the past, your marital pattern, your family of origin, and your personal development. In five or six workbook sessions you will begin to develop a much deeper understanding of your marriage and how each of you contributed to it. At this point, you probably think you know everything there is to know about each other and why we work together the way we do. I promise you, you are in for a surprise!

After the affair forgiveness process, the workbook will help you both to turn and face the other direction—toward the future. Beginning with chapter 5, you will begin to move toward developing the kind of marriage you've always wanted. The workbook will help you save what is valuable (the restoration) and assist you as you develop new skills (the enrichment). This is the fun part of the recovery process. You still might have some bad days, but the frequency and the number of good days will definitely be on the upswing.

In chapter 7, you will begin writing what we call "The Final Project." This paper consists of four chapters; it will bring together all that you have learned about yourself, your marriage, your future, and the family you came from in such a way that you will feel like closure is definitely happening to this tragic experience. You won't be finished with this experience quickly; what you need to complete the process is time: time to heal, time to develop different patterns, time to rebuild trust, time to let go of old hurts, time to build new history, and time to share with family and friends the good progress the two of you are making.

I say "friends" because I believe that God will bring into your life somebody who needs the kind of help you have received from going through this process. If you happen to be a Christian, God gave His promise that He comforts you for the purpose that one day you will be prepared to comfort someone else with the very same comfort that you received from Him (2 Corinthians 1:3–4).

About Homework

This workbook is built upon daily twenty-minute homework exercises, initiated by each spouse on alternating days. The homework will include touching exercises, monologues in which one spouse listens to the other, and dialogues. (See appendix A for a complete list of assignments.)

If the spouse refuses to initiate the homework but is willing to do the exercise with you, then do the exercises only on your days. Do not allow yourself to be put into the place where you are initiating all the homework. Recovery from infidelity is a two-way street.

The workbook provides training in five skills necessary for a good marriage.

1. *Feeling Identification:* The ability to identify clearly not only what you are feeling but also the intensity of that feeling and the words to express it.
2. *Communication Structure:* A fair way to speak and to be heard, designed to make both spouses feel safe in their roles of either listening or talking.
3. *Conflict Resolution:* The ability to resolve differences and the ability to tolerate any currently unresolvable issues.
4. *Spousal Spiritual Practices:* The development of a bonding beyond yourselves, a sense of purpose/mission for your marriage, the development of a genuine soul mate.
5. *Nonsexual Touching Exercises:* The ability to express affection and care with

physical touch that doesn't lead to erotic or sexual activity, the kind of nurture that initially bonds couples together, and which is commonly replaced with sex as the marriage matures.

Written exercises are brief and to the point. Neither of you will be asked to do a lot of introspection. Your marriage is in a crisis, and energy, the ability to concentrate, and time are all at a premium.

Each chapter has a theme. Order is important; do not skip ahead or jump around. The exercises are designed to build upon each other in a certain sequence. Some chapters are exclusively for the infidel and should be read only by him/her. The spouse (i.e., the one who did not "stray") will hear the information in those exclusive chapters; the goal is for you to hear it from your husband/wife.

THE CONTRACT

I said earlier that this workbook will help stabilize the marriage so that you can make appropriate decisions for your family. The contract below is a commitment to this process. It is *not* a commitment to the marriage. If you are uncertain about staying in this marriage, you must still sign the contract committing to this process. Make your-selves clear to each other: you are only committing to this process. This is essentially the same contract that the couples I work with are asked to sign, and this is the same introduction that I give them.

The purpose of having a contract is to help keep you engaged in the process when the going gets rough. It will become difficult, but the ten to fifteen weeks that you invest in this process will be forever viewed as helpful regardless of whether or not you save the marriage.

CONTRACT FOR TORN ASUNDER CONTENT

The following information is meant to clarify the recovery process you are considering entering into.

General information:
Time frame: 10–15 weeks
Review at session 6 or 7 with option to terminate should any party desire to do so
Weekly meetings, with one-hour sessions per meeting
No contact of any kind with partner during time period committed to counseling
Cannot initiate divorce proceedings during counseling period

Counseling tasks include, but are not limited to:

- Identification of six (6) core issues (3 from each spouse)
- One session devoted to resolution of each core issue
- Interpretation of Marital Satisfaction Time Line
- Identification of individual contributions to the marital deterioration
- Structured forgiveness exercise for individual marital contributions
- Identification of components of sexual indiscretion(s) with structured forgiveness exercise
- Identification of the shared good and bad history of the marriage
- Homework exercises assigned during the counseling period (approx. 20 minutes a day)
- Communication homework exercises must be done face-to-face if in the same geographical location.
- Readers will be exposed to four (4) different communication skills: monologues, spousal-selected monologues, dialogues, and nonsexual touching exercises
- The completion of the four-chapter Final Project

Process:

This is not considered typical marital therapy—it does not focus on current interaction patterns and does not provide individual therapy.

Purpose:

To stabilize the relationship (not save the marriage) in the aftermath of the disclosure of infidelity

I have read the above material and agree to abide by the stated conditions.

_____ _____   _____ _____
Signature: Husband　　　　　　Date　　　　　　Signature: Wife　　　　　　　Date

_____   _____
Print Name　　　　　　　　　　　　　Print Name

The Marriage Atmosphere

There is much more information in the textbook (see chapters 1 and 9 of *Torn Asunder*), but clearly the two of you will have multiple, intense, probably late-night conversations in which one or both of you are on the verge of leaving the marriage. If you will just stay dedicated to this difficult work, in about six or seven weeks you will sense that those conversations are diminishing in both frequency and intensity, and that there are more good days between the bad times.

SPECIAL CIRCUMSTANCES

As you prepare to begin this workbook and the process of review and possible restoration of the marriage, you and your spouse may need to address several special circumstances. Here are four of note.

Sexual Testing

Sexual testing (i.e., for sexually-transmitted diseases [STDs], including AIDS) is required of the infidel. Regardless of how safe you think you have been with the partner (i.e., "the other woman/man"), you must be tested. It will alleviate anxiety and in most cases takes the issue of STDs out of the picture. While waiting for the results, all sexual activity in the marriage should be done only with protection. Take nothing for granted.

Should the infidel test positive, seek sound medical advice, no matter how minor the infection might appear to be. And, of course, tell your spouse in order to help him or her as well.

Legal/Financial Issues

Sexual harassment is on the rise, and in some careers individuals can lose their license to practice their specialty if they have had affairs with their clients, patients, or coworkers. This potentially compounds the recovery process with multiple losses. It also distracts from the marital issues and often makes financial survival the primary goal. In many of these cases, it causes the spouse to defend the infidel as he/she tries to save their family income.

If you find yourself in this circumstance, it is probably not wise to begin this workbook until the career issue is settled. If the career settlement appears to be a long, drawn-out affair, then the two of you will have to adhere to strict guidelines as you work through the anger and hurt of the affair while in the midst of the anger, fear, and hurt of the income loss.

Pregnancy

This is the most complicated special circumstance of all, and you will need legal advice as you work through this issue. If the partner becomes pregnant, there will be financial obligations toward the child, and usually visitation requirements. Adoption issues often surface, and there will be an entire series of staying-in-touch-with-the-partner rules. This child, and its resulting financial and visitation requirements, create a bond with a partner that most marriages cannot tolerate.

As a general rule, any financial transactions between the infidel and the partner should be handled by a third party; for example, a banker, an attorney, a pastor, etc. Any further contact between infidel and partner is pure poison to the recovery process; you need to strictly adhere to this point.

Need for Disclosure

If the spouse is not yet aware of the affair, you need to do this section first. It would be wise to read the text of the book *Torn Asunder* (chapter 12) for a full discussion of the benefits of telling your spouse. This can be a scary time, especially for the unfaithful one. Indeed, the infidel's greatest fear is disclosure. Below is a chart for the infidel to consider. It will help you sort through the ambivalence you have of sharing this painful secret. Fill it in and see what you think of the outcome.

Disclosing the Affair

If I Tell . . . _____

Best Case: _____

_____

_____

_____

Worst Case: _____

_____

_____

_____

If I Tell . . . _____

Best Case: _____

_____

_____

_____

Worst Case: _____

_____

_____

_____

This material is adapted from Emily Brown, *Patterns of Infidelity and Their Treatment* (New York: Brunner/Mazel, 1991).

The fear of this disclosure is itself a high hurdle to clear for the infidel. But, having put your thoughts down in writing will be helpful to both of you as you initiate the recovery process. Usually the actual worst case is not nearly as bad as the imagined worst case; putting it in black and white often calms your fears.

Imminent Divorce

Perhaps you got hold of this workbook with divorce imminent—maybe even already filed. Let me remind you that much of what this workbook does for couples is going to be necessary for you and your spouse even if you do eventually divorce. You still will have to rebuild trust in each other. If you have children, you will be working together for years, and trust is essential. There also will be financial exchanges between the two of you, and times that you will need to ask favors of each other. This workbook can be helpful for both of you, even if divorce appears to be the outcome at this time.

Fleeing a marriage "just" because of adultery (and by no means do I minimize the seriousness of adultery) causes a spouse to drag all the unfinished business of this first marriage into the next relationship. Even if divorce is the result of this affair, you both need to finish off this marriage first. Work through forgiveness. Rebuild your trust. Sort through the good and the bad of this relationship. Understand why this affair happened and take the prevention that you learn with you into the next relationship. This workbook will help you do just that.

I promise that you will not experience pressure in this workbook to stay in the marriage. These exercises will not be a guilt trip for you. I earnestly believe that if you decide to work through the tough issues outlined here, you will be glad you did, regardless of whether you decide to divorce or rebuild.

At this point, you may be anxious about even working through the exercises in this workbook at all. That's OK; it's quite normal in fact. If this is the case, just journal below what your fears are.

The fears I have about doing this workbook: _____

_____

_____

_____

_____

Telling the Children

Your children feel the tension going on in the home right now. They will make up their own story about what is taking place, and often that can be worse than reality. Therefore, you need to tell them. They need reassurance and comfort. Tell them only the truth, and do it together.

Go ahead and explain any "new rules" that have resulted from the affair; don't let them remain unspoken. Such new rules might include Mom and Dad sleeping in separate bedrooms for a time; or that the children should expect crying spells (or silent periods) and to not let those tears rattle them, etc. Do provide some framework for this process that the two of you are going through. Do share responsibility for the deterioration of the marriage and don't blame one party exclusively for the affair.

If they are teenagers, they fully understand adultery. You don't need to share the gory details, but you don't need to hide the fact of adultery either. Your children have plenty of friends whose parents have committed adultery and who have gotten divorced. For more age-specific suggestions, see "What to Tell the Kids" in the main book (pages 293–96).

Enlisting Support

Both of you need a same-sex friend to help you through this stage with support, prayer, listening, and so forth. Accountability is helpful, but in some cases not healing. This affair is between the two of you, not any third parties; it has an emotional component that accountability groups cannot fix and often do not want to deal with. Most accountability structures are concerned only with thought processes and behavior. Controlling your spouse's behavior is not the issue, otherwise one of you will always need someone else in your marriage to "manage" the other. This friend must be able to keep confidences, must be able to listen, and must not have any delusion about "fixing" either or both of you.

Key Concepts for Recovery

During more than thirty years of helping husbands and wives recover from infidelity, I have found that several critical concepts have aided couples in surviving this catastrophic marriage event. You may find some of these concepts not easy to swallow; in fact, you might have quite a reaction to them. That's OK. But give careful thought to the frequency of their acceptance in couples who recover fully before you abandon them. In addition, be sure to read chapter 4 of the book *Torn Asunder* before you proceed with this chapter of the workbook. Please read those pages now.

In this chapter, you will receive your first homework exercise, the "Marital Satisfaction Time Line." You'll come face-to-face with the issue of divorce and the freedom each spouse has to stay in—or leave—the marriage. If you are the infidel, you will be faced with numerous questions that you must answer frankly and openly. You will assess the affair pattern, you will consider the personality and history of the "other woman/man" involved in this marriage, and last of all, you will learn some techniques for anger management and recurring depression issues.

Now let's look at some of those difficult yet crucial concepts mentioned earlier.

Shared Contribution

The most common form of marital deterioration is one to which both spouses have contributed. The subsequent marital infidelity is what I call the "entangled affair," or "Class II affair." In this workbook, we will not be concerned with the exact percentage of each spouse's contribution to a marriage's fracture, and neither of you should be, either. Arguing over who contributed more to the destruction is useless toward rebuilding this marriage. What's done is done, and now you must spend your energy on processing the past and building for the future. It is necessary to acknowledge a shared responsibility so that each spouse has equal influence to shape the marital outcome, the future pattern. If you see the affair as the sole fault of your spouse (as though you were perfect), you will have no influence over the future shape of this marriage. How can you improve upon perfection? Do not let your spouse either blame you completely for the affair or, conversely, assume total responsibility for it.

We need a balance here. As a marriage deteriorates, both spouses are at risk for infidelity. It is just a matter of time to see who falls first. Each of you has had "close calls," and by admitting it could have been you, instead of only the infidel, you help level the playing field.

Spouses less than happy with the marriage send out signals that give off news of their dissatisfaction. There are interested individuals out there who are "scanning" for these signals, both men and women. No one ever forced a spouse to have an affair at gunpoint; rather, both of you contributed to a marriage pattern which made an affair almost inevitable.

Having said that, let me add this truth: If you're the spouse of the infidel, realize *you don't need the infidel any longer.* A premature commitment to the marriage at this point will stifle the work necessary for recovery. You are free to leave the marriage. Jesus said so (Matthew 19:3–9). You must see yourself as free to leave, so that you can make a choice whether to return to the marriage and to not come back merely because you feel obligated to do so.

Asking Questions

The faithful spouse has a right to know the answer to every question he/she has asked. It is important to bring secrets to the light. If this marriage stands any chance of being saved, both parties have to fully know this bit of their *shared* history.

Often the infidel seeks to protect the spouse by sharing information in a guarded or careful manner. To continue this behavior will make it almost impossible to rebuild trust between the two of you. It is too late to be careful, to be "discreet." At this point "discreet" sounds like "dishonest" to the spouse. Share exactly what the mate asks for—no more, no less.

To the faithful spouse I would say that even given all the painful information you learn about the affair, your task is to forgive and let go of your urge to seek revenge, to hurt the infidel back. On the other hand, I'm not saying that you should keep your head in the sand; being ignorant is not the answer. Rather, you need to eventually give up your need to exact payment from the infidel.

With that in mind, both spouses need to address the fears they feel about asking and disclosing information about the affair. Please complete the appropriate blanks about your fears.

For the spouse: My fears about asking—

_____

_____

_____

_____

For the infidel: My fears about telling—

_____

_____

_____

_____

CAUTION: *Infidel:* If you force your spouse to ask the "perfect question" in order to receive the answer they are looking for, you will be perceived as hiding something and there will be no trust as long as this perception exists.
Spouse: Remember, the infidel was "drunk" with infatuation. An individual in this state does not always recall sequences perfectly. They often don't remember details. There is difficulty in recalling experiences. Just remember what it was like when you had an inappropriate crush on someone in junior high or high school: The world stood still, you forgot to do your homework, you were lost in the dream world of "love."

It is common for the spouse to become obsessed with certain details and questions, asking the same ones over and over. The person is looking for a reason to either ease a lack of awareness prior to the disclosure or to provide justification for the affair. Some obsessing can be normal and OK, but it can also be overdone. If this obsession lasts more than two or three weeks, it will become a defensive posture, keeping a spouse from working on his/her own issues and causing the recovery process to bog down.

On occasion, *after* the marital fact-finding process, specific questions may need to be asked. If so, here is a ritual that often proves helpful to both spouses.

When the urge to ask a specific question arises, the spouse is to ask God out loud in prayer if this question is permissible to ask of the infidel and then wait for an answer from God. For example, the spouse would say, "God, I am going crazy wondering how my (wife/husband) _____ (insert here the action that is agonizing to the person praying) with the partner without me knowing. Is it important for me to know this to heal our marriage?" It is amazing how well this works, and it makes the process safe for both spouses.

The Purpose of the Marriage

A second key concept for the spouses to understand is the purpose of their marriage. Why did you select each other in the first place? There are two primary assumptions here:

1. You were *not* psychotic when you chose each other (although probably both of you at one time or another have said that to yourself!).
2. Most Western marriages are not arranged by parents. (Wouldn't it be nice to have somebody else to blame right now?) Therefore we must assume sole responsibility for choosing the other.

It sounds self-evident, but spouses in crisis often forget why they did choose each other. Here are some common reasons—see if some of them fit your pattern.

Maybe you made your choice to:

- Round out your individual shortcomings
- Finish off a family-of-origin relational deficit
- Heal pain existing at the time you met each other
- Provide escape from some current problem or difficulty
- Feel needed or necessary for your spouse's existence or development
- Find someone different than yourself to complete you

Maybe your spouse offered you a needed factor, such as security, time, money, or status. Whatever the reason, it has proven insufficient to keep your marriage safe from infidelity. You need to identify the original reason(s) for your selection so that you can determine some new purpose, later on, for reconciling this marriage. You have space below to record what were some of your purposes for selecting the spouse you did.

What are some of the reasons I chose you to be my spouse?

1. _____
2. _____
3. _____
4. _____

Personality and History of the Partner

This is the only section of the work that will look at the partner, "the other woman/man" in this affair. Understanding the partner is a key concept; it can hold some important clues as to why and how the affair took place and can even assist in the forgiveness process. Be warned: It will be painful.

Often the partner has a long history of promiscuity, a personality prone to this kind of pattern, and has demonstrated that they are better at what they do (through repeated seductions) than the infidel was at what she/he did (resisting temptation). This discrepancy in abilities doesn't make it easier for either of you, but it will help in the understanding of how this affair happened.

Write about your feelings if you think any of this is true of the partner. Then write why you think it is true.

_____

_____

_____

_____

> C A U T I O N : When a wife has been unfaithful, often the husband would like to view his wife as being seduced—which is really another way of saying she's innocent in this affair. Be careful of jumping to that conclusion. It might be painful to admit that she was a willing partner, but the truth is what matters. No one held a gun to her head, and this fact must be embraced by husbands (or wives, for that matter) who offer this objection to admitting the truth.

The Partner's Personality Patterns

Some personality patterns, especially those of some females, are prone to act out sexually. This workbook is not the time or place to explore all this, but if you suspect this to be true of your circumstance, I strongly suggest that you read *The New Personality Self-Portrait* by John M. Oldham, MD (Bantam). The first few pages of that book include a survey that your spouse and you can fill out on the partner to see if he/she matches the personality pattern prone to infidelity. Your scores will point you to the right chapters to read in that book. While you are at it, take the survey on both yourself and your spouse. This information will be quite helpful in an assignment that appears later in this workbook.

The Partner's History

Was this the partner's first affair? Did the partner get over this affair with the infidel by getting involved in another affair? Did the partner pursue the infidel? Was the infidel aware of this pursuit? Did the spouse sense this pursuit and voice caution about it early on? (This might make the forgiveness process a bit more difficult.) Write out your responses to these questions below:

_____

_____

_____

The Partner's Marital History

Individuals involved in affairs have a tendency to criticize their spouses. Who started the kind of provocative conversation that led to this affair? It could have been the soon-to-be infidel, the partner, or both. At this point, let's focus on the partner. Did the partner see his/her spouse as "all bad" and the infidel as "all good," or perfect, "meant for each other?" Was the infidel drawn into this relationship to help the partner with his/her bad marriage?

Write below some factors in the partner's background, and the interaction between the infidel and partner, that may have played a role in this affair.

_____

_____

_____

Though painful, this kind of information is important to talk about together.

CAUTION: Sometimes the infidel perceives the need, at least early on in the recovery process, to protect the partner. The infidel feels responsible for some of the pain that he or she generated in the partner's life and might even feel an obligation to reimburse the partner for expenses he or she might have incurred during the affair. This is usually a huge source of anger to the spouse. If this is some of what you are experiencing as a couple, write about it below and share with each other later.

_____

_____

_____

Concerning the above caution, keep in mind this process of recovery will never be fair. In fact, the faithful spouse will have to "pay" for this affair twice—once at disclosure and again through this painful recovery process. So, in a sense, this is just the way it is, even though it feels inherently unfair.

Anger Management and Depression Concerns

Anger management is one of the largest issues you will deal with; the main book has an entire chapter devoted to the topic ("Anger in Affairs," chapter 9), with some exercises that are often helpful to the spouse. One of the exercises that can be incorporated here is to write out one's feelings as opposed to acting them out. Write out your feelings below, and also have an additional journal available, since it is doubtful that these few lines will contain all your feelings! If you are unable to share them with your spouse, maybe a same-sex friend would be available. Let it all out.

_____

_____

_____

_____

_____

One of the signs of the relationship's return to health is when the infidel finally feels that he/she has the right to get angry or irritated again at the spouse. Initially, most infidels feel like they deserve everything that is dished out to them, that they have no "legs to stand on" when it comes to a disagreement. Yet to continue to allow this practice escalates the spouse's apprehension, who fears driving the infidel back into the partner's arms. It is always healthy to write about your anger prior to talking about it. Later in the workbook, you will begin a dialogue model that will allow you to process the anger in a safe environment.

Both spouses will go through bouts of depression in the recovery process. Depression robs the individual of energy that is desperately needed to focus on the work at hand. Sleep disturbance especially is a concern. The mental confusion, the short-term memory loss, the decrease in productivity, the increasing fear of not making it—these all cooperate to rob both individuals of the strength to go on. Often the short-term additional use of an antidepressant medication is very helpful. If either of you finds yourself spiraling downward, it might be wise to seek a physician for some help. Most of the newer antidepressants take several weeks to be fully effective, so don't wait until you get to a point from which recovery is going to be difficult.

CAUTION: The infidel's depression often is due to a loss of his "medication," that is, the mood-altering experience he/she found in being with the partner. A good illustration of this is in the Old Testament story of Samson and Delilah. Samson knew that Delilah was trying to kill him, but he could not stay away from her. She made him feel better than normal, and he continued to see her in spite of the danger to himself. In the first few weeks after disclosure, the infidel does not feel normal and often yearns for that euphoric feeling that the partner provided. Actually the depression is a good sign that a healthy separation process is taking place. This is especially true if the infidel felt "in love" with the partner.

You might want to read the book text where the grieving process is described as alternating between the two of you (pages 136–39). There is also a discussion about how to best care for each other during this time.

How do you think you and your spouse are doing in the anger and depression areas? Write your thoughts below.

_____

_____

_____

_____

_____

_____

Having a Monologue

Now we begin the monologue process, a technique that has benefited many couples. A monologue occurs when you sit *knee-to-knee,* and one person talks for twenty minutes nonstop. The other spouse gives full attention to the presentation but is not allowed to ask questions, make comments, or evaluate in any way what is being said by the talking spouse. A watch (or a timer on the microwave) is a good way to maintain the twenty-minute time. When the twenty minutes are over, the two of you separate and let the conversation "percolate" in each of you. Much like the old percolating coffee-makers moving water through the coffee grounds, reflect and absorb the comments. Let them drip through your life experience; don't react right away.

Occasionally, if you are both enjoying the monologue and mutually agree to do so, either spouse may continue beyond the twenty-minute guideline. Later on in this workbook, you will be given some additional instructions for "tweaking" this model; but for now, keep it a simple monologue.

A Monologue

The topics are biographical in nature. Below is a list of topics that you can use to stimulate your recall for this discussion.

- The homes you lived in
- Your bedroom appearance
- Your schools; favorite and worst teachers
- How you spent your allowance and other money
- How your family celebrated holidays and birthdays
- Family vacation
- Pets
- How you spent your afternoons after school
- How you spent your weekends
- Favorite TV shows
- Best/worst decisions, experiences
- Best/worst dreams, pastimes
- Earliest memories (from birth to age nine)
- Chores
- Relationship with friends during this period
- Relationship with relatives during this period
- Sunday morning activity at your house
- Your family car during this period
- Parental conflict—over what and when
- Mealtimes at your house

This list is not set in stone; you may add anything of a biographical nature to this list. Your first monologue will be from birth to nine years of age; the second monologue from ten to fifteen years of age; and the third monologue from sixteen to twenty-one years of age. In this last monologue, you will want to add age-appropriate experiences like part-time jobs, proms/dances, cars, college experiences, and sports teams you played on. One of you will do the monologue birth to nine on Monday; the other spouse birth to nine on Tuesday; the first spouse will do ten to fifteen on Wednesday, etc., until you complete the biographical monologue.

Below you can write some ideas that you want to bring up when it is your turn.

Birth to Nine Years:

_____

_____

_____

Ten to Fifteen Years:

_____

_____

_____

Sixteen to Twenty-one Years:

_____

_____

_____

Marital Satisfaction Time Line (MSTL) Exercise

Here is your first homework exercise. This will take some time, so get out the old photo albums and have lunch or dinner with your spouse as you work on it. You will complete a separate sheet of paper for each five years of marriage. Each spouse will have a complete set (e.g., if married thirty-five years, each of you will have seven pages), so each would photocopy seven empty time lines for this exercise. You will fill out the bottom squares identically. You can do this one of two ways: Either fill out one set (usually used when one person's handwriting is more legible than the other's), and photocopy a second set; or you can each write your own set, but you must do them together and they must be identical.

In the boxes at the bottom of the chart, note all the significant events in your marital history, such as:

- Births
- Moves
- Deaths
- Health issues & major illnesses
- Any marital difficulty
- Counseling experiences
- Significant vacations
- Job promotions or losses
- Major accidents

- Financial/legal issues
- Any living situation that included people beyond your nuclear family
- Any significant pets
- Any significant hobbies

Make sure you place the same events in the same box. The dotted lines represent six-month markers, the solid lines represent year markers. Be sure to put the respective year in the smaller; box to show a clear chronology. After you have the history recorded in the boxes, get some privacy (i.e., work separately from each other). Individually then, place one dot on each vertical line that would represent your marital satisfaction at the time the events in the box below (attached to the vertical line) were taking place. Though your current circumstances might make it difficult for you to recall any of your marriage as "good," you must put yourself back into that time period and ask, "How would I have rated that time period back then?" Connect the dots and tape the sheets together to develop a time line. In the next chapter, you will use this time line to sort through your marital history and the likelihood of saving this marriage.

Marital Satisfaction Time Line

Name _____ Age _____ Years Married _____

Rating
High

5

4

3

2

1

Low

Years

© Dave Carder

Looking at Your Marital History

I t's time to take a helpful look backward at your marriage. The review of the Marital Satisfaction Time Line (MSTL) will provoke all kinds of discussions, many of which could last into the wee hours of the morning. I encourage you to listen to each other. I know you are going through tremendous emotional upheaval, having good and bad days—and even good and bad hours right next to each other. You are right where you should be, even though it doesn't feel very good right now. Stay in the process, keep on working, and you will get through it.

One instruction prior to beginning this workbook chapter: Please read chapter 5 of the book *Torn Asunder*.

Before the Joint Review

Now pull out your individual time line and lay it in front of you. Complete the following checklist:

❍ Make sure you have a dot on each vertical line expressing your satisfaction level at the time of the activities listed in the attached box.

❍ Make sure all the "dots" are connected so that a time line becomes apparent across the marital history.

❍ Make sure all your sheets are taped together.

❍ Finally, does the time line reflect your honest recall of the marriage and should any dot be adjusted prior to your spouse seeing your chart?

CAUTION: If this is a second marriage for either spouse, check yourself to see if the ex-spouse or the first marriage is "flavoring" the current MSTL.

Joint Review Time

Now, with forty-five minutes to an hour of uninterrupted time, get together with your spouse, lay both MSTLs on the floor in front of you and begin to talk, in overall terms, about what you see. Be alert to your very first impressions; often they are the best. Make sure you ask any questions you have in order to fully understand what your spouse has identified. Do not hurry through this process. It is the accumulation of all the years you have been together; it doesn't deserve to be rushed.

During the review of the MSTL, *make sure you listen.* Do not try to correct your spouse's recorded perceptions. This is a time for each of you to explore how the other has viewed your history. Don't be defensive. Remember, this is a picture of the old marriage, not a prediction of how the new marriage will look.

As part of the review time with your spouse, complete the following sections, including "resiliency" and "The First Five Years."

Overall Impressions

- How did you feel about doing this exercise?
- Are you surprised by some of your spouse's satisfaction levels?

_____

_____

_____

_____

Similarities

- How similar are your charts?
- Do they have the same "flow"?
- Do they record similar dips and peaks at the same time in response to the activities in the box?

_____

_____

_____

_____

Emotional Tone

What does the "emotional tone" of the marriage look like? Is it a:

- "Flat line"—boring, predictable, functional?
- "Low level"—with little nurturance going on, interaction is task-oriented?
- "Slope"—is in decline across the life of the marriage or varied, representing normal highs and lows of married life?
- "High, level, flat line"? This often represents a spouse who has few expectations of the marriage and who is self-contained, without need of the spouse.

_____

_____

_____

_____

Resiliency

What is the history of resiliency in your marriage? Answer these questions:

- Have satisfaction levels ever hit bottom and recovered?
- Was the recovery satisfying and sufficient for both spouses?
- What encouraged the recovery process?
- If there was a slow recovery, why?
- Finally, what has happened to the satisfaction levels since disclosure?

_____

_____

_____

_____

The First Five Years

Most couples report a high level of satisfaction in the early years of the marriage. If one or both of you do not have scores in that range, this needs some discussion beyond what you might have yelled at each other in the past during a fight. For instance:

- Do you report other high-level satisfactions later on, and at the same time?
- What made them good?

- Is there any pattern to how long the high-level periods last?
- Do you both agree on why the low level of satisfaction is apparent at the beginning of the marriage?
- If so, do you both agree on what could have been done differently to elevate the satisfaction levels of the early years?

_____

_____

_____

_____

CAUTION: Since research strongly suggests that the first five years do set the tone of a marriage, it is important that you work through these questions. Don't shy away; do the hard work.

Save the MSTL Charts

You will want to come back to these charts periodically through the recovery process. You will also find them interesting to review at the end of this process, and to possibly share with friends and family later on. You might find that some of your spousal-selected monologues will come back to the content of the MSTL.

Predicting Recovery

Most couples want to know right up front what chance they have of recovering fully from this affair and moving on with their lives.

The following is the best clinical statistic I can provide. It is not supported by hard research, but it does have an anecdotal base; many couples report it to be the case in their marriages. My experience over the past twenty-five years suggests the following guideline: It appears that couples who have at least 20 percent of their marital history at levels 4 or 5 _simultaneously_ (i.e., both spouses report the same satisfaction levels during the same period) and _chronologically connected_ (it cannot be six months here, six months there, etc.; all 20 percent has to be contiguous) will have a greater than 90 percent chance of staying together. Not only stay together, but within the next two years they will be able to say to each other, "This is the best our marriage has ever been, even better than I thought it ever could be."

Now I am quick to add that if your MSTL does not match the 20 percent profile, it does not mean that you cannot survive infidelity. What it does mean is that it will require you, as a couple, to do much more work than the couple whose profile does make the 20-percent minimum. This brings into focus the fact that this is *tough work*. Frankly, if your high-level satisfaction falls below 10 percent of your history, it is going to be next to impossible to save the marriage. In a marriage with little history of high satisfaction, there is not much left to save. The good news is that it can only get better. But it is so much easier for couples who have some good history to fall back upon as they try to climb out of this pit.

Special Circumstances

The Bipolar Marriage

The 20-percent pattern doesn't tell the whole story on this subject; there is a "good marriage" pattern that doesn't meet the criteria of the 20 percent due to its repeated periods of instability. I call it the "bipolar marital pattern."

In this marriage pattern, the couple has frequent up-down cycles of very good periods followed by very bad ones. They find it difficult to string together the good times long enough to meet the 20-percent minimum in terms of continuity. However, the good periods (levels 4 and 5) when added together equal more than the minimum necessary to predict a satisfactory outcome. Invariably, the affair has happened during one of the low-level periods.

If your pattern reflects this description, the two of you will need to change a number of your interactions to enhance your stability. The volatility of your relationship predicts a repeated affair if you maintain your current pattern. For you, it's not just a matter of getting over the affair, but a radical transformation of the marital interaction that you've put together through the years.

Note below some patterns that may exist in your marriage.

_____

_____

_____

_____

The Post-Trauma Affair

In the post-trauma affair, the primary, and often only, trigger is a discussion of some recent trauma by the soon-to-be-infidel with the future partner. It could be a death, a major job dismissal, a medical diagnosis with severe implications, difficulty with an adolescent resulting in family upheaval, etc. Any trauma that the spouse feels he/she cannot talk over with the mate can be the starting point. Often, the inhibition of talking with the spouse is due to a desire to protect the spouse who is viewed as already overwhelmed, exhausted, or worrying too much for any additional conversation to take place. Dialogue is held back out of fear that it will be "the straw that breaks the camel's back." Trauma highlights spousal differences. Some want to talk it through, others become stoic, still others split it off and try to go on. Some spouses might withdraw and hide. Some will automatically gravitate to friends and family for comfort. Any of these patterns can keep spouses from supporting each other, thus creating vulnerability to infidelity. If you feel the affair in your marriage fits this category, do the following exercise:

What trauma triggered this affair?

_____

_____

_____

_____

What was going on with the spouse during the initial stages of this trauma?

_____

_____

_____

_____

What attempts to process this trauma were made prior to the affair?

_____

_____

_____

_____

For a full discussion of affair types, please see the *Torn Asunder* book, chapters 2 through 4. It will be very important for the two of you to agree upon the type of affair that has occurred in your marriage.

HOMEWORK

All of us bring numerous relationship interactions from our family of origin into our marriage relationship. Most of these interactions have never been examined; they are automatically transferred to the next relationship, the marriage. The homework in this chapter will help you identify three significant areas of the interaction in your family of origin.

You will also have the opportunity as the talker to ask for "feedback." Feedback is not an evaluation or a criticism, but rather an affirmation, an observation, or some other form of positive support. As the listener in the following three monologues, you must keep the environment safe if your spouse is going to open up to you. Be careful of storing up what you hear to use later against your spouse. Do not use what you hear to validate your perception of what has gone wrong in your marriage. Rather, just listen and learn as your spouse walks you into his or her life as a child. Use the same format as you did before in the biographical monologues.

First Monologue: Family-of-Origin Conflict Resolution Practices

How did your family of origin resolve differences? What rules did they use and require of the children? Following are some common rules/practices:

- Some families run away from anger entirely, lest they say something they later will regret.
- Some family members can be verbal with anger; others can physically hit people or things.
- Some members are allowed to knock holes in walls or slam doors.
- Some families have different rules for the males and females in the family.
- Some families "select" one person to be angry all the time—to express the anger for everyone else in the family.
- Some families see anger as sin and don't tolerate differences of any kind.
- Some families say in effect, "Smile; pretend like it doesn't bother you."
- Some families act like conflict doesn't bother them but retaliate when the other least expects it.

What were the primary rules about anger and conflict in your family of origin?

_____

_____

_____

What role did you play in the family interaction?

_____

_____

_____

What role did each of your parents play?

_____

_____

_____

What role did each of your siblings play?

_____

_____

_____

Who had the most power in your family?

_____

_____

_____

How did that person maintain it?

_____

_____

_____

Is this still true today? Why or why not?

_____

_____

_____

How do you think this has influenced you today?

_____

_____

_____

Is the influence the same at home as it is at work (outside the house)?

_____

_____

_____

Are you practicing the same pattern with your family, your spouse, your children?

_____

_____

_____

If you could change your present pattern, what would you like to change?

_____

_____

_____

Did you ever wish it was different when you were a small child in the family?

_____

_____

Second Monologue: How Old Am I on the Inside?

This monologue has to do with your internal age versus your chronological age. Rarely do they match perfectly across the life span. Here are ten sets of questions; I have found with couples the most effective way of doing this monologue is to first prepare your responses by writing out the answers.

How old do I feel today?_____
Why? _____

_____

_____

What is the idealized age I would like to return to?_____
Why? _____

_____

_____

What was the biggest gap (and at what age did it occur) between my internal age and my chronological age? _____
Why? _____

_____

_____

Did I ever "get stuck" internally and stop growing?_____
Why? _____
_____
_____

What makes me feel older on the inside than what I am chronologically?
_____
Why? _____
_____
_____

How old was I on the inside when I met my spouse? _____
Why? _____
_____
_____

Have I continued to grow and develop like I should? _____
Why? _____
_____
_____

How do people in authority make me feel on the inside?_____
Why? _____
_____
_____

When I'm around my parents, how old do I feel? _____
Why? _____
_____
_____

What person makes me feel older/younger? _____
Why? _____
_____
_____

Third Monologue: Parental Influence in Our Marriage

This monologue is concerned with the family-of-origin influence on you. For most of us, the marriage we grew up in is the only marriage we really know much about. As a result, we often unconsciously fall back upon that pattern that we know best, the one we lived in. This exercise will give you and your spouse an opportunity to identify those influences, to rate your own satisfaction with your current practices, and to guess how satisfied your spouse is with this routine.

Sometimes an adult child takes the whole collection of his or her family values, beliefs, practices, and attitudes into the marriage, thus causing the spouse to feel married to a family and not to an individual. At other times a spouse will tend to ignore that attachment, knowing intuitively that to bring up the subject only invites marital discord. Most of us can see our in-laws in our spouse's behaviors and we will use the accusation, "You are just like your mother" or "You are just like your father" in a derogatory way to highlight our concerns. This is not helpful, so here is another way to discuss the same topic.

Monologue: Parental Influence In Our Marriage

As you fill out this review, remember the purpose is to share it with your spouse face to face. Only jot notes sufficient to remind you of what you want to share. Keep in mind that many marital interactions are a response to or a reaction against what one experienced in their family of origin. The issue is not "is this a good or bad practice," but rather, "are we both happy with it, or are we just behaving this way because my parents did/did not do it this way."

Behavior Roles	Primary Responsibility		My Own Satisfaction	Spouse's Satisfaction
	Marriage	Family of Origin	Rate: 1 2 3 4 5	Rate: 1 2 3 4 5
Cars			1 2 3 4 5	1 2 3 4 5
House			1 2 3 4 5	1 2 3 4 5
Cleaning			1 2 3 4 5	1 2 3 4 5
Household Chores			1 2 3 4 5	1 2 3 4 5
Cooking/Menus/ Food Purchase			1 2 3 4 5	1 2 3 4 5

Behavior Roles (cont.)	Primary Responsibility		My Own Satisfaction	Spouse's Satisfaction
	Marriage	Family of Origin	Rate: 1 2 3 4 5	Rate: 1 2 3 4 5
Childcare			1 2 3 4 5	1 2 3 4 5
Home Maintenance			1 2 3 4 5	1 2 3 4 5
Yard Maintenance			1 2 3 4 5	1 2 3 4 5
Remodeling/ Decorating			1 2 3 4 5	1 2 3 4 5
Bills/Financial Mgmt.			1 2 3 4 5	1 2 3 4 5
Schedules				
Who gets up first			1 2 3 4 5	1 2 3 4 5
Who gets to stay up late			1 2 3 4 5	1 2 3 4 5
Who gets up first with children			1 2 3 4 5	1 2 3 4 5
Who makes sure home is secure			1 2 3 4 5	1 2 3 4 5
Who gets to sleep in			1 2 3 4 5	1 2 3 4 5
Who gets to enjoy their hobbies first			1 2 3 4 5	1 2 3 4 5
Whose friends matter most in family schedules			1 2 3 4 5	1 2 3 4 5
Values			1 2 3 4 5	1 2 3 4 5
Who spends money			1 2 3 4 5	1 2 3 4 5

	Primary Responsibility		My Own Satisfaction	Spouse's Satisfaction
Schedules (cont.)	Marriage	Family of Origin	Rate: 1 2 3 4 5	Rate: 1 2 3 4 5
Who saves money			1 2 3 4 5	1 2 3 4 5
Who has most discretionary income			1 2 3 4 5	1 2 3 4 5
Who is Responsible for				
Family Spirituality			1 2 3 4 5	1 2 3 4 5
Couple Closeness			1 2 3 4 5	1 2 3 4 5
Sex			1 2 3 4 5	1 2 3 4 5
Family Activities			1 2 3 4 5	1 2 3 4 5
Family Scheduling/ Shuttling of Children			1 2 3 4 5	1 2 3 4 5
Relationships/Atmosphere			1 2 3 4 5	1 2 3 4 5
Children's Homework			1 2 3 4 5	1 2 3 4 5

1. Items where I follow my Family of Origin (FOR) practices:

2. Items where I do the opposite of my FOR:

3. Items I wish we would practice now like my FOR:

4. My impressions after looking over my responses:

5. My impressions after sharing with my spouse:

Three Primary Issues

From the work done above, your personal experience of the marriage, and the recent affair, each of you needs to identify three primary problems that exist between the two of you. Answer the following question:

What three things need to change in this marriage for me to stay in it and be happy?

1. _____
_____
2. _____
_____
3. _____
_____

These issues need to be brief. They need to identify specific interaction patterns between the two of you. The word *happy* has been chosen on purpose; God intended marriage to be a delightful experience, and not drudgery to be tolerated. Indeed, that is why most couples choose each other—they used to be happy!

These issues will become the focal points of the dialogue process later on in the workbook. However, you can talk about these selections anytime you want, using "I" messages in the monologue format and leaving the word *you* out of the conversational pattern.

Prayer Exercise

You'll be given three different kinds of prayer exercises to do in this workbook. The first exercise will take approximately three to five minutes daily. It's very simple and it will help you express concern for your spouse in the midst of all this turmoil.

First, each of you will take a 3 x 5 card and write three simple requests on it about yourself. They can be any kind of requests. The requests cannot be about the children, your job, schedules, money, etc.; remember, they have to be about you. Second, you will exchange cards. By receiving your spouse's card, you will be saying, "I will pray for your requests three times a day." A spouse can change the requests at any time, but he or she can only have three requests on the card.

Praying for your spouse doesn't take much time at all; you can do it while you shave, drive, cook, work, etc. Just pray for your spouse according to their self-declared needs, three times—today. And tomorrow. Remember, though, that you are to do this exercise every day. Pray for your spouse daily. Begin it today, and continue for the next thirty days.

You must do this basic prayer exercise for the first thirty days. The second thirty days will have a different prayer exercise (explained in chapter 6). You are certainly encouraged to talk anytime about answers to prayer, how you feel about doing this exercise, etc. It is always good to talk about answers to prayer.

Marital Style

Research has identified four marital styles, or patterns, that are especially susceptible to infidelity.[1] These marriages usually have hidden issues that have not been addressed by either spouse. Spouses might not even be fully aware of the issues or the patterns that have emerged in the relationship until an outside partner offers an alternative. The old pattern has to change, but first the two of you have to identify the components that created your style.

One instruction prior to beginning this workbook chapter: Please read pages 68–74 of the book *Torn Asunder*.

Begin this chapter by attempting to identify your marital style through the following exercise. If, after you do the exercise below, you still have not identified a marital pattern, don't worry; there is an additional set of exercises later in this chapter dedicated to helping couples uncover their particular marital interaction pattern.

Exercise: Marital Styles Prone to Infidelity

Circle the number you feel represents the level of each trait within your marriage. Then total the numbers at the bottom. Let 1 represent rarely, 2 occasionally, 3 regularly, 4 frequently, and 5 most of the time.

Intimacy Avoidant — "The Windshield Wiper Marriage"

1 2 3 4 5	• Open conflict. Picking on each other, teasing
1 2 3 4 5	• Keep each other at arm's length
1 2 3 4 5	• Low-level nurturance in marital relationship
1 2 3 4 5	• Project-oriented, looks efficient and effective
1 2 3 4 5	• If one partner does something (including infidelity), the other will also, to keep it "balanced"
1 2 3 4 5	• Push each other's buttons to "check out" if system is still intact
1 2 3 4 5	• Everything looks good to those outside the family

TOTAL: _____

Conflict Avoidant — "The Dial Tone Marriage"

1 2 3 4 5	• Little disagreement, no conflict allowed
1 2 3 4 5	• No differences tolerated, "look-alike"
1 2 3 4 5	• Fixed, efficient roles for everyone in the family
1 2 3 4 5	• Tendency to be too enmeshed, putting off outside attachments
1 2 3 4 5	• Look perfect, do everything as a family
1 2 3 4 5	• Very little emotion expressed
1 2 3 4 5	• Parent/child relationship between spouses

TOTAL: _____

"The Empty Nest Marriage"

1 2 3 4 5	• Sacrificial, heroic support of and focus on children
1 2 3 4 5	• The marriage feels empty, boring, quiet
1 2 3 4 5	• Little effort and money spent to maintain marriage
1 2 3 4 5	• No dating, little money spent on spousal relationship
1 2 3 4 5	• Satisfaction derived from family happiness
1 2 3 4 5	• Spousal emptiness surfaces when children begin to depart
1 2 3 4 5	• Affair is always a big secret, with a reluctance to disclose; infidel doesn't want to be seen as bad guy

TOTAL: _____

"The Out-the-Door Marriage"

1 2 3 4 5   • Departure planned years in advance, even on honeymoon

1 2 3 4 5   • Loyalty in marriage is to children

1 2 3 4 5   • Desire to be single

1 2 3 4 5   • Affair is simply a way out of marriage

1 2 3 4 5   • If pursued, infidel threatens to marry the partner

1 2 3 4 5   • Departure is after twenty-year relationship, children
1 2 3 4 5   gone, military service, civil service, retirement, etc.

1 2 3 4 5   • Concern for spouse being left

TOTAL: _____

You and your spouse should add your two scores together. Any pattern that receives a score close to 60 or above is the pattern the two of you have developed over the years. This pattern helps identify the specific interactions and attitudes that need to change in the "new marriage." The style will become a hot topic of discussion between the two of you. (For more information on these patterns, read chapter 3 in the textbook.)

> CAUTION: During the affair, the infidel often begins to view the marriage as all bad, always unhappy, and the spouse as never having been loved. That perception will provide a false positive score for the out-the-door marriage style; in other words, since the infidel has convinced himself that he "never really loved" his wife, seeking an outside partner as a way to get out of the marriage is only logical. To you, the infidel, try to evaluate the marital pattern the way you perceived it prior to the affair.

Now, each of you alone, work through your pattern by completing the items under "Our Pattern" and giving consideration to how these factors contributed to the breakup of your marriage. First, decide which of the four patterns discussed above, if any, would fit your marriage; list that under "Pattern." Then list the primary characteristic(s) within each pattern that typified your marriage (for example, if the wife's primary loyalty was to the children, not the spouse, under "Out-the-Door," list that).

The vast majority of those I counsel do find one of these four patterns that fit, but some do not find any. If you are in the latter category, turn to the next section, "Unlisted Marital

Style," and complete the exercises. The items there will provide fodder for you to discuss this facet of your recovery; then come back and do the written exercise shown below. Even if you have determined your marital pattern, be sure to complete the "Unlisted Marital Style" exercises as well. It will be very enlightening about your interactions with your spouse.

Our Pattern

Pattern: _____

Characteristic(s): _____

_____

_____

What I liked and didn't like about this interaction: _____

_____

_____

How I contributed to its development in our marriage: _____

_____

Where I think I saw it practiced (i.e., modeled to me) prior to meeting you: _____

_____

_____

_____

_____

_____

What dynamic caused me to maintain this pattern with you: _____

_____

_____

_____

Unlisted Marital Style

For those of you whose scores were not high enough to clearly identify one of the four patterns listed above, here are some great exercises for each of you to work through independently. When finished, compare your results with those of your spouse. Then privately complete the exercise "Our Pattern."

For those of you who did identify with one of the four styles, you too can benefit from working through the following exercises. These are just another way, or angle, to get at the same material in your marriage that the four classic styles represent. Much like many facets on a diamond give a better overall view of the gem's clarity, color, and brilliance, so many different ways to examine the marriage help us to better view—and repair—the marriage. You may learn that a different pattern exists and thus revise the style you tentatively identified in the previous exercise.

CAUTION: Initially you might see the style quite differently from the way you view it after some interaction with the material and each other. Practice some give-and-take here, and try to come up with an interaction pattern you both agree on. If you still need help, ask close friends for their review of your marital style along with the notes you and your spouse have put together. Remember, this is not a review of how it should be, but rather how it really has been for the two of you in your marriage up until this point.

Marital Focal Point

This exercise focuses on the OK topics and the taboo topics of the old marriage. Examples might be that it was OK to talk about work, but not OK to talk about dissatisfaction in the sexual relationship. Personalize these to your situation.

When we did talk, we only talked about:
1. _____
2. _____
3. _____

We can't talk about:
1. _____
2. _____
3. _____

Marital Dance

Similar to the previous exercise, the following material highlights the "dance" that perpetuates the unhappiness in the old marriage. Couples often develop point-counter-point responses that do not solve anything; they only prolong the agony. Examples might include, "When my spouse raises his voice in a disagreement with me, I go into hiding and nurse my anger toward him" (instead of sharing it openly). Personalize these.

When my spouse _____, I _____
When my spouse _____, I _____
When my spouse _____, I _____
When my spouse _____, I _____

Marital System

Enlarging upon the "dance" concept, this diagram shows four phases, circulating in a clockwise direction, starting at the top center, "The Problem." It could also be called "The Marital Merry-go-round." It is a self-perpetuating cycle. Though the phases are labeled assuming the woman's response and then the man's reaction, etc., the gender labels could equally be the other way around. Fill in your particulars, and use separate paper if you want to "map" other issues. (Once you get the hang of it, you probably will want to!) On subsequent maps, reverse the gender labels where appropriate.

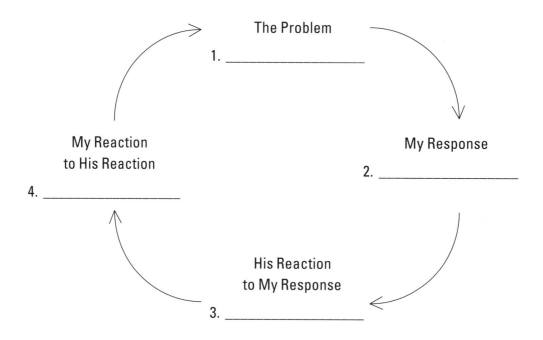

The Problem

1. _____

My Response

2. _____

My Reaction
to His Reaction

4. _____

His Reaction
to My Response

3. _____

Contributions, Opposites, and Behaviors

As you continue to uncover your marital style, *determine the contributions each of you make* to the marriage. Some examples would be, "I provide all the money, she provides all the spending." Or, "I provide all the housework, he provides all the TV watching." Adapt these to your situation.

I provide all the _____; my spouse
provides all the _____.

I provide all the _____; my spouse
provides all the _____.

I provide all the _____; my spouse
provides all the _____.

....

Opposites attract, and nowhere is this plainer than in marriages. Ironically, it is often true that a personality trait that initially is attractive to a mate later turns out to be the chief irritant. Examples here would include, "I am punctual; she is always late." Or, "I am fun-loving; he is a workaholic." Go for it.

I am _____; my spouse is _____ .

I am _____; my spouse is _____ .

I am _____; my spouse is _____ .

....

Here we identify behaviors that help and hurt marital intimacy—the kind of soul-mate bonding we all need but so few of us enjoy. List the behaviors that bring you closer—and drive you apart. We provide only three work spaces for these paired behaviors, but if you find more, by all means use additional paper. Examples might include, "We get close when I initiate sex; we move apart when I want to just talk." Or, "We get close when I buy you flowers, we move apart when I watch all nine football games on TV every weekend." Remember, these are only "I" statements—no blaming allowed!

We get close when I _____ .
We move apart when I _____ .

We get close when I _____ .
We move apart when I _____ .

We get close when I _____ .
We move apart when I _____ .

You now have identified your marital style and highlighted the items you want to change about your contribution to this "old marriage." You will have multiple opportunities to discuss these with your spouse. They are never off-limits.

This has been a fairly complex set of exercises. However, most couples who do this work find it incredibly enlightening. Here comes the challenge for the two of you: *Name this pattern.* Be creative, because it will become a "code word" that either of you can use in the future to call attention to the times when you feel like you're slipping back into your old pattern. Once you've named the pattern, return to "Our Pattern" and complete the exercise.

> **CAUTION:** Always approach these discussions from the "I" point of view; that is, what I did, and how I kept this practice going, not what your spouse does—or does not do. The word *you* (directed at your spouse) should not appear in these conversations.

HOMEWORK

My Contribution List

Class II and Class IV affairs are always about marital deficits. Part of the reconciliation process involves each spouse admitting these deficiencies. The following exercise takes the focus off the affair and the infidel and places it on the marital deterioration that made the relationship vulnerable—and the affair inevitable. This exercise is difficult for both spouses and should be done in private without any input from one spouse to the other. Each of you will be working on your faults in the marriage. Remember, to err is only human; no one is a perfect spouse.

To do this exercise is not tantamount to saying, "My shortcomings made my spouse have an affair." On the contrary, the infidel is fully responsible for his/her own choices. However, the environment you both helped create in this marriage still exists and needs to be changed if there is to be a future healthy relationship. So, for that reason, the question you both are going to work on privately is: "What did I contribute to the marriage that caused it to deteriorate to the point of infidelity?"

It might be helpful if you would think of your contributions as falling into one of three categories:

- Things you didn't do that you should have done in your marriage
- Things you did do that you should not have done in your marriage
- Accidental items

Accidental items are those experiences or circumstances that were so overwhelming, that in the process of surviving, you neglected your marriage. An example might be the tyrannical boss who requires unpaid overtime just to maintain the job; or a chronically ill child that consumes the parent, day and night, who is trying to provide the required care. No one would choose to live in an experience like this. Furthermore, the "wrongness" that needs confession in experiences like these is not the behavior, but the spouse's inability to keep the marriage as a priority. Thus a confession in this circumstance would read, "I was wrong when I let the illness of our child consume me to the point that I neglected our relationship."

	Area	*Elaboration*
1.	_____	_____ _____
2.	_____	_____ _____
3.	_____	_____ _____
4.	_____	_____ _____
5.	_____	_____ _____
6.	_____	_____ _____
7.	_____	_____ _____

Be honest here. There is nothing left to save in the marriage, so go ahead and bare your soul. This is a great opportunity to clean up a lot of baggage that you both have accumulated through the years. Most spouses easily identify seven to ten items. If there is a longstanding hurt in the marriage, make sure it shows up on this list. Work on your list over two or three days. When you've done this, consider the following commonly reported areas of contribution. Check to see if some of them should be added to your list:

- *Money.* Spending too much; controlling or attempting to account for every penny; money secrets; hidden accounts, etc.
- *Sex.* Not responding to or initiating sexual activity; boring sexual patterns including frequency; same kind of sexual love-making; lack of emotional involvement; lack of teasing and touching.

- *Power/Control.* The use of intimidation, anger, jealousy; demanding an account for every second spent away from the spouse; secrecy with long periods unaccounted for, demeaning and cruel speech.
- *Fun.* A loss of fun in the marriage; the failure to take responsibility for having fun; giving in to too much responsibility; recent refusal to spend money on fun. Remember: Most couples marry to have more fun together, not less!
- *Nurturance.* A loss of caring for each other; failure to provide tenderness, sympathy, appreciation for each other; a tendency to become self-absorbed, thus withdrawing emotionally from spouse; moving in separate worlds.

Did any of these last five areas strike an additional chord in your thinking process? If so, add them to your list.

	Area	*Elaboration*
1.		
2.		
3.		
4.		
5.		
6.		
7.		

Now that you have finished making out your contribution list, you have one final exercise to do in private. While sitting alone in a chair, pull an empty chair in front of you, pretend your spouse is sitting in it, "show" them your list, and ask them if there is anything else they think you should write down. If nothing comes to mind, you are done with your contribution list.

You are probably wondering what's going to happen to this list. In the next chapter you will develop it into a forgiveness letter; stay tuned.

Infidelity can never be paid for. There isn't a ransom available to satisfy the betrayal, the hurt, and all the pain that accompanies this experience. Forgiveness is the only way to take care of it.

Note

1. These four types of affair-prone marriages were first identified by Emily Brown in *Patterns of Infidelity & Their Treatment* (New York: Brunner-Mazel, 1991).

Preparing for and Processing Forgiveness

This chapter provides preparation for forgiveness. Often the spouse of the unfaithful mate feels uncertain about forgiveness at this point; it might appear to be too early, and thus "cheap." There is fear that the infidel has not suffered enough; there is apprehension that marital change might stop and regression or stagnation might occur. Sometimes the spouse feels that the wound is too fresh and the pain too recent for forgiveness.

In this text, neither of you will be forced or pressured to forgive too quickly. In fact, I would encourage just the opposite: Forgive only at the pace that feels comfortable to you. As you actually prepare for the reading of the forgiveness letters, you'll be given three very clear options that will provide you with freedom-of-response choices.

Before proceeding with this workbook chapter, please read pages 220–24 of *Torn Asunder*. (I also highly recommend reading and applying *The Five Languages of Apology* by Gary Chapman and Jennifer Thomas, Chicago: Northfield, 2006.)

First, let's look at what forgiveness does—and does not—mean:

- Forgiveness does *not* mean that the two of you cannot get angry about the state of the marriage or about the affair in the future. (I can assure you that just the opposite is true!)
- Forgiveness does *not* mean that the two of you cannot talk about the affair anymore. You both will talk a lot about it for months.
- Forgiveness *does* mean that the spouse is not going to hold the affair over the infidel any longer. Holding the affair against the infidel is the same as "I can make the

infidel pay" for the affair. This is folly. Remember, there is no means available for the infidel to pay for the affair.

- Forgiveness *does* mean that the spouse is willing to "fess up" to his/her contributions to the marital deterioration that allowed the affair to flourish in the first place.

Having said that, let me acknowledge that the spouse can rarely forgive the affair at the first reading of the affair forgiveness letter. The pain is just too fresh. It is also true that the spouse easily pays twice in this forgiveness process—once at disclosure and again throughout the recovery process. Thus forgiveness has an inherent sense of unfairness to it, but it is the only path that brings healing to both parties.

Prior to the actual reading of the forgiveness letter, each of you will be given clear instructions. The spouse being asked to forgive will receive several choices that include the option of delaying forgiveness. So, as you proceed in this chapter, do so without reservation. You are in a safe place!

This chapter will provide instructions for two different forgiveness letters—one for the person's contributions to the marriage that caused it to deteriorate to the point of infidelity (both spouses), and one for the affair itself (infidel only). (This last section should be read only by the infidel.)

Fears about Forgiveness

We all have a forgiveness history that began in our family of origin and continued to develop in our marriage. That history certainly influences and often contaminates our forgiveness practices. It will continue to do so until you individually have sorted through it all. Below are some exercises to help you do just that.

What has been my experience with forgiveness? _____

_____

_____

Have I been easily forgiven? Do I forgive easily? _____

_____

_____

Have the ones who have hurt me quickly identified their wrongdoing and corrected their behavior? _____

_____

_____

Have people in my past apologized and only used it as an escape from punishment without changing their behavior? _____

_____

_____

What are my three greatest misgivings about this whole forgiveness process?

1. _____
2. _____
3. _____

Two other factors, besides your personal forgiveness history, will influence the level of forgiveness that the two of you will experience: first, your definition of the word *forgiveness* and secondly, your theological or religious orientation towards forgiveness. To help you identify how you view the forgiveness process, look at the list of words below and circle two that you feel most closely reflect your definition of forgiveness. This might be helpful to talk over with your spouse prior to actually going through the forgiveness exercise.

Forgetting	*Condoning*
Pardoning	*Accepting*
Excusing	*Letting go*
Reconciling	*Moving on*

One of you may view forgiveness as automatically leading to reconciliation. Forgiveness is viewed as a trap in this case, but let me remind you that forgiveness is going to be required if you don't want to become bitter and if you are to salvage your children from this devastation. This forgiveness involves both spouses and is not the duty of just one person. To facilitate forgiveness, the offender must be specific about what they did that hurt their spouse, identify how that behavior affected the spouse, make a clear request for release from the consequences of the grievance, and create an awareness that they will not do this intentionally in the future.

We have all had the experience of thinking we have apologized only to find out later, sometimes much later, that the apology was ineffective. Why does that happen? Because people have different languages of apology. Chapman and Thomas remind us that some folks need to hear expressions of regret ("I am sorry"), others, acceptance of responsibility ("I was wrong"), still others want restitution ("What can I do to make it right?"), while some need to see and hear repentance ("I will try to not do that again").

Finally, almost all of us need to hear a request for forgiveness ("Will you please forgive me?"). (See *The Five Languages of Apology,* Chapman and Thomas.)

The following forgiveness letter draws upon several languages of apology. But knowing your spouse like you do, you might need to "tweak" your letter a bit to highlight what you know is important to her. Think carefully about this. Remember, you are attempting to facilitate forgiveness, so say what she needs to hear in order to help her let go of this.

The Forgiveness Letter

This letter may at first appear too brief, maybe even cold and clinical. Don't worry, that is exactly the way it should be!

You will use *each of the contribution items* on your contribution list in the first sentence of each three-sentence paragraph. In the second sentence, you will *identify three feeling words* that your spouse experienced as a result of your behavior. In the third sentence, you *will always make this simple request*: "Will you forgive me?"

Using the following illustration as a guide, write your letter below.

Outline:

I was wrong when I (Contribution #1). I know this must have caused you to feel

_____, _____, and _____.

Will you forgive me?

Sample (Wife):

I was wrong when I allowed myself to get too caught up in the children's lives and schedule. I know this must have made you feel neglected, unimportant, and only important to us for your paycheck.

Will you forgive me?

Sample (Husband):

I was wrong when I worked too much and even brought work home at night. I know this must have made you feel unimportant, rejected, and lonely.

Will you forgive me?

Now go ahead and write your own forgiveness letter in private. There's room for ten items from your contribution list. You may have more, or you may have less. Fill it up as appropriate.

1. I was wrong when I _____.
I know this must have made you feel _____,
_____, and _____.
Will you forgive me?

2. I was wrong when I _____.
I know this must have made you feel _____,
_____, and _____.
Will you forgive me?

3. I was wrong when I _____.
I know this must have made you feel _____,
_____, and _____.
Will you forgive me?

4. I was wrong when I _____.
I know this must have made you feel _____,
_____, and _____.
Will you forgive me?

5. I was wrong when I _____.
I know this must have made you feel _____,
_____, and _____.
Will you forgive me?

6. I was wrong when I _____.
I know this must have made you feel _____,
_____, and _____.
Will you forgive me?

7. I was wrong when I _____.
I know this must have made you feel _____,
_____, and _____.
Will you forgive me?

8. I was wrong when I _____.
I know this must have made you feel _____,
_____, and _____.
Will you forgive me?

9. I was wrong when I _____.
I know this must have made you feel _____,
_____, and _____.
Will you forgive me?

10. I was wrong when I _____.
I know this must have made you feel _____,
_____, and _____.
Will you forgive me?

Reading Instructions

After you both have finished writing and if you are ready to read your letter to your spouse, set aside a minimum of one half-hour with no interruptions to do so. You will also need some downtime after the reading to reflect on what you have both heard and read.

Prior to reading the letters, read through the following instructions together. Discuss and make sure that you agree on them prior to the reading process.

- The infidel reads his/her letter first.
- Sit facing each other, close enough to touch each other.
- Read slowly and read only what is written. Do not ad lib.
- Make eye contact as often as possible, especially at the last phrase of each item when you ask for forgiveness.
- Each of you is free to ask your spouse to reread any item in the letter. (Sometimes it is cleansing just to hear your spouse acknowledge a shortcoming that has hurt you for years.)
- On occasion, a spouse correctly identifies a wrong behavior, but misidentifies the feelings that the behavior generated in their spouse. If that happens, the hearer should say to the one reading the letter, "I want to talk about the feelings." Clarification is good and necessary, but don't let it become a roadblock in the process. Don't let that lack of understanding get in the way of forgiving that behavior if you are able to do so.
- Each of you will have three response choices to every forgiveness question at the end of each item:

1. "Yes, I will forgive you."
2. "No, I cannot forgive you."
3. "Not now; I cannot forgive you now, but I am working on it."

- At the end of the reading, each second and third choice items (i.e., "no" and "not now" responses) should be reread. Sometimes a spouse can forgive a particular item more easily after hearing the entire list read.

When you have finished reading *and received forgiveness*, reach across and hug your spouse while telling them "Thank you for your forgiveness."

Then exchange letters. Having the letter will be a reminder of your spouse's admission of wrong and your need to forgive those as-yet unforgiven actions. Keep in mind that any unforgiven items now become the responsibility of the spouse who at present can't forgive those items. It will be up to that spouse to notify the other when they are able to forgive the action. The confessing spouse does not have to ask again.

CAUTION: Forgiving an item does not mean it will never happen again, but it does mean that the behavior will not happen again intentionally. By putting this item in the letter, the spouse is saying, "I know this is wrong and I know it is hurtful, and I won't do it again on purpose."

HOMEWORK

After both spouses have read their letters, separate for a time and reflect on what you have just said and heard. Write out your feelings to the following questions:

How do I feel having gone through this exercise?

_____

_____

_____

_____

_____

_____

_____

_____

What other areas of confession would I have liked to have heard from my spouse?

	Area	*Why*
1.	_____	_____
		_____
2.	_____	_____
		_____
3.	_____	_____
		_____

What feeling words (identified in my spouse's letter) do I need to clarify for him/her to have a more accurate understanding of how this behavior affected me?

	Item	*My Response*
1.	_____	_____
		_____
2.	_____	_____
		_____
3.	_____	_____
		_____

What will have to happen before I feel I can forgive the items I responded to with a "no" or "not yet"?

	Item	*Need*
1.	_____	_____
		_____
2.	_____	_____
		_____
3.	_____	_____
		_____

Time for a Monologue

Later in the week, but prior to the reading of the affair forgiveness letter, you should present your responses to the above questions as a twenty-minute monologue time. Your spouse should do the same the next day. Remember that as a monologue, you present your material twenty minutes *nonstop*. Your spouse simply listens. No questions or comments by the listener are allowed.

Affair Forgiveness Letter

CAUTION: We begin with the caution first. If the affair forgiveness letter does not apply to you, please do not read this section. Only the infidel should complete this section. If the spouse, because of curiosity or whatever other reasons, "trespasses" on this section, the process of reconciliation will be greatly hindered. Thus, if you are the spouse of the infidel, you should skip to the "Follow-up Exercises for Spouse after the Affair Forgiveness Letter Is Read." At the end of the week, when you feel ready, you can ask your spouse to read this letter to you. At that time, you will have the same three response choices to complete, and the same reread pattern will apply.

If you are the infidel, you have several exercises to go through prior to constructing the affair forgiveness letter. The better job you do on the front end, the better the outcome. First, ask yourself, "Is my spouse a generalist or a detailed person?" If your spouse is a detailed individual, then you will need to be detailed when you identify your behaviors and activities that you are asking her to forgive. To do otherwise will sound like you are discounting what you did wrong and there won't be much relief for either of you. I would highly recommend that you read *The Five Languages of Apology* by Chapman and Thomas prior to going through this exercise.

Second, list all the behaviors and activities for which you want forgiveness. Take a couple of days for this part of the exercise. Pray, ask for insight. Remember, the more you bring out into the open, the less influence this history is going to have on you in the future. As you construct this list, it is not uncommon for the infidel to recall some activity that the spouse is unaware of, but for which he desires forgiveness. If that happens to you, tell your spouse about the experience prior to including it in the affair letter. It is not fair to the spouse to hear the behavior for the first time and then immediately be asked to forgive.

After you think your list is complete, rank the items from "least offensive" to "most offensive." Obviously, you want to facilitate forgiveness, so put the "least offensive" items first in the affair forgiveness letter. Prior to reading the letter, tell your spouse about this organization outline so she won't be so anxious about what she is going to hear.

Below are some common items found in most every affair. This will help you get started, but please don't restrict yourself to just these behaviors. Make sure your content fits your experience.

- Listening to and fantasizing about another individual
- Cultivating a platonic friendship with the partner
- Extending the friendship time you can have with the partner
- Lying to cover the time spent with the partner
- Robbing the marriage of emotional energy, e.g., through loss of time together, saving up conversational topics for the partner, emotionally withdrawing when physically present with the spouse, and refusing to be sexual with the spouse
- Spending money on the partner
- Developing special codes, songs, rituals with the partner
- Taking the partner to places the marriage had experienced or that the spouse wanted to visit
- Criticizing the spouse and the marriage
- Contaminating the "sacred" (having sex with a partner in "our" car, bed, at our special places, and/or in our special ways)
- Being sexual with the partner (this includes all sensual/erotic behavior, not just intercourse)
- Making plans with the partner about the future
- Embarrassment the affair has caused the spouse with friends and family
- Injuries to the children that have occurred as a result of the affair

You might have other items that need to be included in your list.

In the blanks below, you (the infidel) should write a second affair forgiveness letter. The letter will be in precisely the same fashion as you wrote the previous letter: your contributions, three feeling words, and a request for forgiveness. This second letter is unique in its point of view; it's from the viewpoint of the one who strayed.

Here's a sample of the content: "I was wrong when *I listened to and began to fantasize about the partner.* I know this makes you feel *sad*, *abandoned*, and *unwanted*. Will you forgive me?" Now complete the letter, using the form on the next two pages.

Your Affair Forgiveness Letter:

1. I was wrong when I _____.
I know this must have made you feel _____,
_____, and _____.
Will you forgive me?

2. I was wrong when I _____.
I know this must have made you feel _____,
_____, and _____.
Will you forgive me?

3. I was wrong when I _____.
I know this must have made you feel _____,
_____, and _____.
Will you forgive me?

4. I was wrong when I _____.
I know this must have made you feel _____,
_____, and _____.
Will you forgive me?

5. I was wrong when I _____.
I know this must have made you feel _____,
_____, and _____.
Will you forgive me?

6. I was wrong when I _____.
I know this must have made you feel _____,
_____, and _____.
Will you forgive me?

7. I was wrong when I _____.
I know this must have made you feel _____,
_____, and _____.
Will you forgive me?

8. I was wrong when I _____.
I know this must have made you feel_____,
_____, and _____.
Will you forgive me?

9. I was wrong when I _____.
I know this must have made you feel_____,
_____, and _____.
Will you forgive me?

10. I was wrong when I _____.
I know this must have made you feel_____,
_____, and _____.
Will you forgive me?

When you're ready and before the end of the week, read the letter to your spouse in the same way you read your "Contribution Forgiveness Letter." Your spouse has the same three response choices, and the same reread pattern applies. When finished, cut the letter out of the book and hand it to the spouse as you say: "With this letter I hand you all my secrets and pray that one day your forgiveness will be so complete that neither of us will remain wounded for life."

CAUTION: Most spouses cannot forgive all the details of the affair this quickly in the recovery process. So expect some "no" and "not now" responses. It will be up to your spouse, though, to tell you when he/she is able to forgive you after the next reread. Do not ask for forgiveness again.

Follow-Up Exercises for the Spouse after the Affair Forgiveness Letter Is Read

After the infidel has read his/her letter, write out your feelings to the following questions:
How do I feel having gone through this exercise?

_____
_____
_____

What other areas of confession would I have liked to have heard from my spouse?

	Area	*Why*
1.	_____	_____
		_____
2.	_____	_____
		_____
3.	_____	_____
		_____

What feeling words (identified in my spouse's letter) do I need to clarify for him/her to have a more accurate understanding of how this behavior affected me?

	Item	*My Response*
1.	_____	_____
		_____
2.	_____	_____
		_____
3.	_____	_____
		_____

What will have to happen before I feel I can forgive the items I responded to with a "no" or "not yet"?

	Item	*Need*
1.	_____	_____
		_____
2.	_____	_____
		_____
3.	_____	_____
		_____

Rebuilding Trust

The biggest question most spouses have in the recovery process is, "Will I ever be able to trust my spouse again?" Sometimes, if the spouse has a history of betrayed trust from childhood, it is almost impossible to rebuild the trust after infidelity. I personally think that is why God provides for the option of divorce after adultery. Sometimes, an individual's history is just too wounded to tolerate another betrayal. Still, even if you find yourself in that position, these exercises will be helpful for you to bring closure to this betrayal. To leave now—without rebuilding your ability to trust in a significant other—will only cause you to drag this most recent pain into your next relationship. So do the work, regardless of whether you expect this marriage to survive.

> CAUTION: If you and/or your spouse are using this workbook to recover from sexual addiction, your progress will be more difficult than that of the couples attempting to recover from the other kinds of affairs. In a Class III (sexual addiction) affair, both spouses have major betrayal issues. Sexual addiction is the medication of choice to heal the infidel's own betrayal history; thus, this type of healing process often requires professional assistance.

Though painful, most couples *can* begin to rebuild their trust in each other. In this workbook, you will go about that process the same way you built the trust between you the first time around, while dating. You will use some of the same activities, follow the same rules, and practice the same patterns.

Before proceeding with this workbook chapter, please read chapter 10 of the book *Torn Asunder*.

Somewhere in this process, the spouse needs to finish forgiving the infidel. It is next to impossible to rebuild trust beyond a certain initial point if forgiveness has not taken place. Granting such forgiveness will, of course, take time; you probably already have said "no" or "not yet" to some of your infidel spouse's requests for forgiveness. Continue to ask God's help to be able to forgive those transgressions against you. Recognize that fuller trust—toward the infidel and toward other people—comes when you are able to forgive the person in all areas. Dealing with trust before you have fully dealt with forgiveness is putting the cart before the horse, so make sure you are making strong progress on forgiveness as you work toward rebuilding trust in the relationship.

The recovery model looks like this: To the degree that you can forgive, to that degree you can start rebuilding respect; to the degree that you can start rebuilding respect, to that degree you can start rebuilding trust; and to the degree that you can start rebuilding trust, to that degree you can start rebuilding love.

Four Concepts In Rebuilding Trust

Trust is built—and rebuilt—on four basic concepts:

- *Structure* (agreed-upon rules): "I know exactly what is going to happen."
- *Safety* (freedom from pain): "I can relax in the other person's presence."
- *Nonsexual touch:* "I won't be taken advantage of."
- *Speech tone and content:* "I can listen without fear of being demeaned."

An infant's first developmental stage is usually called "Trust vs. Mistrust," and often it determines how trusting that child will become of his/her environment. It is a feeling of "I can relax, it is safe here" or "I have caregivers close by who protect me and who will look after my well-being" or "I don't have to be on my guard."

This process also occurs in a dating relationship as couples draw closer to a lifelong commitment. Trust grows to the conviction that "this is the one for me" and the couple finally make vows to seal their selection. Their interactions have grown increasingly more intimate and exclusive over time. They say things to reach each other and tell secrets to each other that they would never share with anyone else. They are trusting each other. You learn how to do it the first time in infancy without a choice of whom you have to learn to trust, and you do it a second time when you make a mate selection. You will now do it a third time as you work through this workbook. All trust is built the same way.

Four Rules In Rebuilding Trust

The four basic rules to rebuild trust are:

- *No surprises.* This removes hypervigilance.
- *Informing prior to the fact.* You keep the spouse informed. Don't wait for your spouse to hear of last-minute changes.
- *Keeping your word.* You are where you say you will be, doing what you say you will do, and keeping deadlines, no matter how simple.
- *Not keeping secrets.* In tone and content, there is no guardedness, no hiding.

Though these rules apply primarily to the infidel, they also fit all of us, all the time. Such rules not only rebuild trust, they maintain it. Feelings can arise of *There is no slack.* He may think, *I have to be perfect.* In one sense that is true, in that after this big blow, the infidel is on a stricter-than-normal standard. That's just the way it is. But consistent compliance with these rules will help you move through the trust-building cycle more quickly. Let's take a look at each of the rules separately.

No Surprises

After any betrayal, individuals feel jumpy, overly cautious, anxious, and even paranoid. This cluster of feelings is often called "hypervigilance," that heightened sense of needing to check everyone and everything twice. It is a constant scanning of the environment in order to anticipate not only what is, but also what could happen. It is a form of self-protection from another experience of being "bushwhacked." This stress generates a more sensitive "startle response." The spouse not only jumps more quickly, but also jumps to more extreme conclusions more quickly. In military jargon, the spouse is somewhat shell-shocked, or gun-shy. This is a reasonable reaction to the trauma that has just exploded into his/her life. But don't worry—the startle response will return to normal, given enough time and a lack of surprises.

In this brief exercise, identify what might be some "surprise" areas common to your marriage and what needs to be done to correct them.

Surprise Area   Correction Needed

1. _____   _____

2. _____   _____

3. _____   _____

Informing Prior to the Fact

This rule is a corollary to the no surprise rule above. Basically, if something changes—if you're not going to be where you said you would be, if something takes more time to do than you thought, or if something changes in your plans—don't wait until after your spouse has found out about it to notify him/her. Don't even wait until the last minute, hoping that things will work out for the best. Rather, let your spouse know prior to the fact. It is a good business practice and it is a good marital practice, especially after a major betrayal like adultery.

In what areas have I often taken liberties like these in the past? (Examples: purchases without telling, working late at night and calling when work is done instead of before beginning to work the extra hours.)

1. _____
2. _____
3. _____

Along these lines, some individuals develop the bad habit of acting first, then apologizing later. You may have heard, "It's easier to ask for forgiveness than to ask permission." This practice might work in certain settings (e.g., the business world), but not now and not in this process.

Keeping Your Word

This is one of the most godlike expressions you have as a human—to declare something and then make it happen. Do not forfeit the influence of this behavior by failure to follow through. Every little statement counts. Do not say something unless you mean it. For example, don't say, "We really ought to get away more often, go to the beach for the weekend or something," if you never really intend to do that. You might think that such a statement will please your spouse and relieve their stress—and it may for the short term. But it will backfire big-time if it becomes yet another betrayal.

Give yourself a "window" of whatever you need in order to meet this requirement. Being faithful in the little things of life is so important here. Examples might include, "Honey, I'll fix the drain tonight after work" or "Tom, I'll sit down and pay the bills on Saturday" or "I'll call you about 1 p.m. today."

This behavior is necessary for both of you to practice. Often an individual feels controlled or stifled by having to comply with what they have said, especially when circumstances change. Nevertheless, *just do what you said you'd do.* Sure, it feels a bit weird, a bit abnormal. But this is not a normal life period or transition. "Normal" will come later.

The tendency to "stretch" what you say is a habit often developed in the family of origin and carried over into the marriage. Reflect on the questions below:

During childhood, where did you see this tendency to "stretch" what one says practiced?

_____

_____

When and how did you first begin to practice this bad habit? _____

_____

_____

How has it impacted other relationships historically—siblings, parents, dating, work, children? _____

_____

_____

In what areas of your marriage has it proven disruptive? _____

_____

_____

Not Keeping Secrets: Voice Tone and Content

Good awareness here provides the same soothing, comforting verbal messages that a mother provides a child. No sharp, agitated, mean speech allowed. It's a conversation with respect, kindness, and gratitude. Generally it is an expression of the fruit of the Spirit (Galatians 5). In fact, it's the fruit of the Spirit and the agape love of 1 Corinthians 13 all rolled into one.

This is not the time to blame your spouse. It is time to talk about tough issues and about the role you see yourself playing in those issues. Focus on yourself and what you do when discussing a difficult subject. Keep in mind that there are two "channels" when you communicate with your spouse: the content channel and the style channel. Sometimes it's not so much *what* you say that hurts (or heals), it's the *way* you say it that counts. Work through the following questions together.

What time of the day is hardest for me to have a pleasant tone and good content: arrival home, mealtimes, mornings, involvement in children's schedules, at work?

_____

_____

What times of the month are the most difficult (business end-of-the-month reports, particular sales periods, Mondays, menstrual cycle, etc.)? _____

_____

_____

What topics are tough for me to maintain good tone and content? _____

_____

_____

About "Being Guarded"

If your spouse feels forced to ask the perfect question in order to get the answer he or she is looking for, you may decimate the trust-rebuilding process. In other words, don't give ultraprecise answers to the question, exactly as it is stated and no more. This is somewhat akin to legal questioning in a courtroom; and it will work well under oath— but it's poison to your marriage. Feeling like enough damage has already been done, the infidel often practices this hypercautiousness in order to protect the spouse from "too much painful information."

Actually, the opposite result occurs: instead of helping the situation, it makes it worse. This infidelity is a part of both spouses' history, not just the one who strayed. Your spouse needs to know this part of his/her own story. The spouse may feel you are being guarded, even if your motive is actually to protect the spouse from pain.

Be forthright and open in your responses. Answer the question clearly. Set aside ambiguity and clichés (and dodges) like "I don't know," "I can't remember," etc. Even when you are truly uncertain about the answer, demonstrate a willingness to explore what happened. Attempt to recall what went on.

If you must, err on the side of too much disclosure, not on the side of too little. To deflect a question only invites mistrust and the feeling that the infidel is hiding something. Don't practice guardedness in an attempt to protect your spouse. Be open; be honest.

Work through the following questions together.

What topics/questions provoke this "guarded" feeling? _____

_____

_____

_____

What is the history of this "guarded" theme in my life? (Many times a child develops this defensive posture to protect himself from punishment or abuse.)

_____

_____

_____

How else, and in what other environments, do I practice this guardedness, e.g., work, social relationships, etc.? _____

_____

_____

_____

What does my spouse do to "get around" this guardedness? How does he or she penetrate it? How do I respond to this process? What would I like to see happen differently?

_____

_____

_____

_____

HOMEWORK

Nonsexual Touching Exercises

As we have seen, a mother builds the ability of her child to trust the environment and the people in it. Without this ability to trust—to trust in your own capabilities, to trust that the environment is "for you" and not "against you," to trust that people respond to you in safe ways—you will not be able to shape your new marriage for the better. It won't be safe to try new patterns.

Just as the child unable to trust (due to childhood abuse) loses his ability to take risks as an adult, so too will you. This whole recovery process involves taking a risk—the risk that if you do decide to rebuild your marriage, the betrayal may happen again.

One of the best ways to nurture this budding trust is to do the nonsexual touching exercises listed below. All are twenty minutes in length, and I encourage you to do them as homework this week and in the following weeks. They will help you to (1) emotionally nurture your spouse and yourself, (2) rebuild trust, and (3) reinforce boundaries.

Remember, these exercises must not lead to intercourse! Though it might sound crass to be so blunt, it's important that this restriction be clear. A large portion of couples in this predicament confuse intercourse with love; that's the whole point of doing these exercises—to learn to associate caring touch itself with love. Giving caring touches *as expressions of love* is very important now. For now, during the rebuilding process, it's very important to keep caring touches and sex separate.

Hand . . . Foot . . . Head

Here are three twenty-minute exercises you can practice this week; each day do a different exercise. The exercises will focus touches to the hand and forearm, foot and leg, and head and shoulders of your spouse.

Before doing the exercises themselves, answer the following questions.

As I read through these exercises, what are my first impressions? _____

_____

_____

Do any of them appear to be difficult to do? Which ones and why? _____

_____

_____

How willing will my spouse feel about this exercise and why? _____

_____

_____

CAUTION: Some spouses resist doing these exercises for a variety of reasons:
- They don't want to nurture their spouse this early in the recovery process.
- They are afraid of being misinterpreted by their spouse.
- The marriage has never had much nonsexual touch and it seems uncomfortable or weird to start now.
- They are uncertain about whether or not they are going to stay in the marriage at this point, and this exercise seems a bit too personal/intimate.

This is a difficult exercise to do or to allow to be done to you when you are mad, hurt, or afraid. For this reason, I deliberately do not assign this exercise until after the forgiveness process is well underway.

Now, however, is the time to start taking the risk to rebuild the trust regardless of your plans about staying in the marriage. These exercises are for you, too; remember what I said earlier about carrying unresolved issues into a future relationship. You need to learn to trust, regardless of whom it is you trust!

Three Touching Exercises

	Exercise One	Exercise Two	Exercise Three
Focus	Hand, forearm	Foot and leg	Head and shoulders
Boundary	The elbow	The knee	The shoulders
Position	Seated beside other, arm resting in giver's lap	Giver seated on couch, with legs of receiver resting on lap	Giver sitting with back against a wall or headboard; receiver lying faceup between spouse's legs, with head on small pillow
Activity	Light, slow, predictable touches	Massage with lotion	Light, slow, and exploratory touches and massage
Time	5 minutes on each side of hand and arm	10 minutes per leg	5 minutes on right side of head, 10 minutes on face, 5 minutes on left side of head

Source: Adapted from Cliff and Joyce Penner, *The Gift of Sex* (Waco, TX: Word, 1981), 141–45.

Negative Thought Patterns

Below is a list of fifty negative thoughts and feelings that often occur before and during the touching exercises. They come from a checklist developed by a northern California research group, BSTG (Berkeley Sex Therapy Group).[1] Look through the list and see if any jump out at you. Especially read through this list after doing a touching exercise either as the giver or the receiver. Then discuss with your spouse those feelings and thoughts that seem to parallel your own.

Place a checkmark in each blank that applies to the thought and feeling that you have said or could imagine saying in doing these exercises.

Script Lines Checklist

_____ 1. I feel uncomfortable.

_____ 2. I think your stroking feels mechanical.

_____ 3. I feel I'm supposed to like everything you are doing.

_____ 4. I am worried about what you're thinking.

_____ 5. That doesn't feel good, but I don't even know what would.

_____ 6. It feels like you're being too careful.

_____ 7. It feels like you're trying too hard.

_____ 8. I resent that you aren't enjoying this more.

_____ 9. I don't know why we're doing this.

_____ 10. I wish it was OK to ignore you.

_____ 11. I feel hopeless about ever turning you on.

_____ 12. Right now my mind is blank.

_____ 13. I wish I felt more like stroking you.

_____ 14. I wish I could enjoy your stroking.

_____ 15. This is a chore for me.

_____ 16. I'm not feeling anything.

_____ 17. I don't feel like talking.

_____ 18. I feel a million miles away.

_____ 19. This seems difficult and complicated.

_____ 20. I feel turned off.

_____ 21. I'm afraid you're going to feel rejected if I don't enjoy this more.

_____ 22. I feel like you need me to be more involved.

_____ 23. I want something, but I don't know what it is.

_____ 24. I don't think I'm going to like anything we're doing today.

_____ 25. I think I'm mostly doing this because I'm supposed to.

_____ 26. I'm beginning to feel impatient.

_____ 27. You seem preoccupied (or far away).

_____ 28. I feel like there's something else I want to say, but it's not in any of these scripts.

_____ 29. I'm afraid I'm not going to do a good enough job.

_____ 30. I'm afraid you're going to be disappointed.

_____ 31. I keep getting distracted.

_____ 32. I wish we could play hooky from this.

_____ 33. My mind keeps going off into fantasies.

_____ 34. I feel obliged to do as much for you as you have done for me.

_____ 35. I'm afraid you are getting bored.

_____ 36. I'm afraid you won't tell me if you don't like something.

_____ 37. I feel like we both have to succeed at this.

_____ 38. I'm feeling lazy, but like I'm not allowed to.

_____ 39. I'm feeling that there's too much I don't like.

_____ 40. I'm afraid of discouraging you.

_____ 41. I'm feeling too finicky.

_____ 42. I'd feel like a pest if I said everything I wanted.

_____ 43. I'd like to take a break.

_____ 44. I'm afraid you'd get mad if I stopped doing this.

_____ 45. I wish this wasn't so important.

_____ 46. I feel like there's something you want, but I don't know what it is.

_____ 47. I feel like I should appreciate what you are doing more.

_____ 48. It feels like something just went wrong, but I don't know what it is.

_____ 49. I can't seem to concentrate on what I'm doing.

_____ 50. I hate these script lines.

All of the items you checked above have a history behind them; explore that history below. On the left, write which of the fifty statements you can relate to (and share with your spouse. If one is not on the list, add it in the statement line.). Then on the right, personalize it: Explore what basis each statement might have in your family of origin, your married life together, etc. Use separate paper if the space below does not suffice.

Statement	*Personal History of This Statement*
1. _____	_____
	_____
	_____
2. _____	_____
	_____
	_____
3. _____	_____
	_____
	_____
4. _____	_____
	_____
	_____
5. _____	_____
	_____
	_____
6. _____	_____
	_____

7. _____   _____
                                 _____

8. _____   _____
                                 _____

9. _____   _____
                                 _____

10. _____   _____
                                 _____

After processing the above, you might be able to see some overall themes emerging about your relationship: what caused the betrayal, what some of the "cracks in the foundation" are, how you might repair these flaws, etc. Try to summarize much of what you discussed. To help you develop some clarity about all or part of your discussions, write such summary thoughts below:

_____
_____
_____
_____
_____
_____

Spousal-Selected Monologues

This exercise is identical to the previous monologue assignment (chapter 4) with the exception that the listening spouse chooses the subject for the talking spouse to talk about. Take turns in this process; one spouse asks about one topic, the other responds on that one topic. Then you can turn the tables. You must give your spouse twenty-four hours advance notice to prepare his or her monologue. You can ask your mate to talk about anything you'd like to hear him speak about in his life. Here are some suggestions:

- Choose a relatively safe topic to start. If you two survive this recovery process, there will be a future time to discuss the riskier topics.
- Among less threatening issues are these: the spouse's relationship with his (or her) parents/your parents, the spouse's attitude toward money, spiritual issues, or work and career issues, and how those attitudes were shaped.

- You might ask about the spouse's one-, five-, and ten-year dreams (in this case, your relationship and your fit in that relationship is off-limits).
- Another good approach is to ask your spouse to prepare a monologue on the following topic: "How I feel I'm changing physically, emotionally, spiritually, and intellectually as a result of this experience."

Many issues will surface in the initial homework exercises. It is easy, in the midst of all this chaos and tumult, to let some wonderful material "float away." Collect a written list of topics, even if you can't ask your spouse to discuss all of them right now. Should you stay married, your relationship will never be more vulnerable than it is now, and as a result, many thoughts, ideas, and questions will surface that will help build deep intimacy later on when you can discuss them.

CAUTION: Do this spousal-selected exercise only after some stabilization has occurred in the relationship.

Note

1. Bernard Apfelbaum, "Ego Analytic Perspective on Desire Disorders," in *Sexual Desire Disorders,* ed. Sandra R. Leiblum and Raymond C. Rosen (New York: Guilford, 1992).

Reconnecting with Each Other

Throughout the workbook, the emphasis has been on how the rebuilding of trust takes time. However, you should not wait to start reconnecting until trust is completely rebuilt. This chapter helps you reconnect by reviewing some of your good marital and personal history. This restoration process begins at the midpoint of the work, and represents a change in direction. Though one of you might still be uncertain about staying in the marriage, the exercises in the next four chapters still should be worked out to bring closure to the old relationship. Regardless of the final outcome (divorce or not), that old relationship is past; a better future relationship is the goal.

CAUTION: The hopeful spouse, the one who wants to save the marriage, will have a tendency to use these next four chapters as a "thermometer" on how the marriage is doing and how the uncertain spouse is feeling. Keep the following in mind:

1. Do not continually take the temperature of this marriage. Every day is different. If you continue or even begin to do this, you will become unsettled and quite anxious. It's like weighing yourself twice a day when you're on a diet, trying to lose weight. The emotional ups and downs can drive you nuts!

2. Do not ask your spouse if he/she is going to stay. Go through this final process, and enjoy each day one at a time. Work on your own anxieties; focus on the goal at hand, and not the future. The future will take care of itself. (See Jesus' words in Matthew 6:34.)

Eight Great Moments

Most marriages have great moments in them, no matter how bad they might appear to be. Part of viewing this marriage correctly is seeking to build the necessary balanced perception, regardless of whether you stay in the marriage or not. If you continue to choose to see your marriage as all bad (so that you can leave it), you will only set yourself up for disappointment in the next relationship. Let yourself see the good side and even enjoy the good memories. Doing this is just being honest, and it does not mean you have to stay married to this person.

> CAUTION: Spouses often read into this discussion a sign that the infidel is "coming home." Don't. Just enjoy the discussion. Be careful of reading more into it than just friends recalling a very good moment shared between them. For now, that's the level of intimacy you are shooting for: friends.

Individually, each of you should make a list of eight great moments in your shared history (your wedding and the births of your children do not count—you need to look harder than that). When finished, merge your lists. Most couples will have three or four items that match. Start with that core, and then each one add one until a list of eight great experiences exists. Then go to dinner, review this shared history, and have some good laughs. (It probably has been a long time since you had those, so enjoy!)

My List of Great Moments

	Experience	Season of the year	Location
1.			
2.			
3.			
4.			
5.			
6.			
7.			
8.			

How do I feel looking at this list? _____

_____

How do I feel about sharing it with my spouse? _____

_____

Our List of Great Moments (Merged)

	Experience	Season of the year	Location
1.			
2.			
3.			
4.			
5.			
6.			
7.			
8.			

How do we feel looking at this list? _____

_____

_____

_____

_____

If the two of you decide to divorce, it is critical that you view this relationship as both good and bad. This balance will prevent either of you from having to look for the perfect, all-good partner in a future relationship. It also will impact your attitude toward each other in a good way, facilitate communication between the two of you, and help lower the tension in the family system of yourselves and your children. All of us individually and collectively have a mix of good and bad, so be careful of casting this marriage in an all-or-nothing color.

If the two of you decide to stay married, this list will become your "restoration project." Just like value is added to an old car or an historic building when it is rebuilt to its original specifications, so too will you both be restored when you rebuild your marriage on its original experiences.

For that restoration project, which begins after you have finished the workbook, you will need to "redo" each of these experiences over the next eighteen months.

By "redoing" I mean go back to the exact place, in the same season of the year, and experience the original great moment. No shortcuts allowed—that only cheapens the final product. If the memory took place in Europe, then go back to Europe! If it was a college football game, go back to the same stadium, same game, same seat if possible. Rehearse what made this memory great. Anyone in the restoration business will tell you that the process is expensive. But (Need I remind you?) it is much more enjoyable to spend this same amount of money on yourselves having fun than it is to give it to attorneys who are trying to divorce you!

Before you leave the "Eight Greats," put an approximate date beside each experience when the two of you could restore each memory.

Love Languages

Besides the restoration process, you are also going to go through an *enrichment* process. The textbook devotes an entire chapter—chapter 8—to the concept of love languages.[1] Suffice it to say here that to protect the relationship in the future, you will have to know your spouse's love language: how to make them feel loved, cherished, special, and close to you.

Since each individual is familiar only with their own love language, each has the tendency to love the spouse the way the individual likes to be loved—usually with bad results! So, do the following exercise on yourself, then share the outcome with your spouse.

Love Languages Exercise: Step 1

List at least twenty activities that make you feel loved. These could be activities that your spouse has done for you in the past; activities that he/she continues to do in the marriage; activities that you have seen or heard other couples do that sound special to you; even activities that you may have seen in a romantic movie that made you say to yourself, "I'd love that." This may even be a wish list of sorts—and the more items on your list, the better. At this point, leave the love language column blank.

Usually the first ten or twelve items come rather quickly. After that it gets a little more difficult to fill in all the blanks. Take your time. Several days might be in order to do this exercise.

	Behavior	*Love Language*
1.	_____	_____
2.	_____	_____
3.	_____	_____
4.	_____	_____

5. _____   _____
6. _____   _____
7. _____   _____
8. _____   _____
9. _____   _____
10. _____   _____
11. _____   _____
12. _____   _____
13. _____   _____
14. _____   _____
15. _____   _____
16. _____   _____
17. _____   _____
18. _____   _____
19. _____   _____
20. _____   _____
21. _____   _____
22. _____   _____
23. _____   _____
24. _____   _____
25. _____   _____

Step 2

Assign each of the above behaviors one of the five love languages shown below. Sometimes a behavior can be classified under a couple of different love languages. Choose the way you like it best. Total the number of times each language appears, and put its score in the appropriate blank below.

_____ Verbal: written or spoken affirmations
_____ Gifts/tasks: token gifts and jobs that cause you to feel that your spouse was thinking of you
_____ Nonsexual touch: hand-holding, back rubs, arm around the waist or on the shoulders
_____ Focused time: just the two of you walking, taking in a movie, dinner out, alone
_____ Erotic: anything sexual, more than just intercourse

Usually individuals have a primary and a secondary love language. Occasionally, as many as three of the five languages have similar or equal scores. Whatever profile you have, this is basically how you like to be loved. When your spouse practices behaviors in the themes of your lower scores, it probably doesn't register with you (except for those specific behaviors you have listed).

Step 3

Predict what you think your spouse's primary and secondary love languages are.

_____ Verbal
_____ Gifts/tasks
_____ Nonsexual touch
_____ Focused time
_____ Erotic

Step 4

Reveal your love language(s) uncovered in step 2, as well as discuss together your list of activities. Specifically, question each other on these forms of expression of love. Use such questions as, "How do you like me to do that?" "When are you free to enjoy that most?" "What is the best memory you have of me doing this?" Make personal notations below.

_____

_____

_____

_____

Step 5

One spouse needs to reduce the top ten on your love language lists to a small card about the size of a business card. Laminate it. (Self-adhesive laminating sheets are available at any office supply store.) Carry each other's card in your wallet (or on your cell phone if you're the electronic type). If you are in need of "Brownie points" or just want to demonstrate your affection for your spouse, remember to love the person as he/she wants to be loved. Pull out your card, pick out one or two items on the list, and go to town.

Step 6

Sometime in the near future, pick one specific day when you will try to do all (or all that are humanly possible) of the items on your spouse's list. This is what you call "topping off the tank." Go for it!

HOMEWORK

Compliment Prayer List (thirty days)

Each of you will need a little assignment book with a wire spiral binding across the top (approximately 2 1/2 by 5 inches). Each day you will use a new page (the book needs a minimum of fifteen pages, and you will make a separate entry on the front and back side) to write a compliment—something you currently like (or at least used to like) about your spouse. Remember, no one forced you to get married, and it is important for you at this juncture to recognize that there is still some good in this person.

Daily, write a compliment at the top of the page for that day. It could be a job your spouse does for you, a meal the mate fixes, a look the mate gives you, the way the mate takes care of himself, his behavior, anything. Do this once a day for a month, thirty entries. The first six or eight are pretty easy, but to identify thirty different items will take some work! After writing the compliment, write two or three sentences about how you feel when you see this behavior in your spouse.

Now comes the hard part. Together, pray out loud with your spouse, thanking God for this quality that you admire in them. This is really much easier to do than it sounds. You don't have to talk about it afterwards, and you don't have to get flowery in your prayer. Keep it simple; just talk to God.

> CAUTION: Spouses, remember to not take the temperature of this marriage. Just because your spouse is saying some nice things about you does not necessarily mean he wants to stay married to you! Enjoy this exercise for what it is, an acknowledgment of good qualities in you. This is something you would do for a friend, and it is not reserved for married couples.

At the end of the thirty days, exchange notebooks. You have a treasure whether you stay married or not. Read it and enjoy it many times over.

The Dialogue Process

Now you are ready to add the dialogue process to your homework exercises. Many couples are familiar with the basic concepts of "I" messages and summarizing, but my experience suggests few couples have practiced this process until forced to do so through a class, a retreat, or a crisis requiring good listening skills. This skill is like any other; it might feel uncomfortable and/or contrived at first. However, don't deviate from the structure; get the fundamentals down first, and then you can "freelance" your way to a style that best suits the two of you.

This is the process you will use to work through the three issues that each of you identified in chapter 2. Most couples can use this model to help themselves, but some couples (especially if the wife is the infidel) will need some additional assistance. (This is due to the usually heightened anger and usually lowered listening abilities of the average husband.) Several national organizations provide couple communication training and have resources in most metropolitan areas (see the appendix). This kind of assistance should prove quite helpful and less expensive than marital therapy. For now, try and follow the steps and see if you can make this work for the two of you.

1. Together read through the dialogue process below, "How to Get Your Point Across…." Make sure you both agree on what is said and how to do what is described. Then look at "The Dialogue" on page 96.
2. Read through the Feeling Words list together at the end of this chapter. Notice the categories and the intensity level of the feelings. Both are important. You are free to look at this list anytime you feel it necessary while in the actual dialogue process with your spouse. (When I first was learning this skill, this sheet became a bible to me.)
3. *Steps 3 and 4 are optional.* I encourage you to obtain and view together *The Dialogue* DVD. Information on securing the DVD appears in appendix B. This is an unedited, live session with a couple I had seen for about ten minutes prior to helping them work through this issue. This is not staged, has no actors, and is a genuine dialogue on a topic of choice for this couple. Only the sound quality has been enhanced. Watch the DVD together following the process on the dialogue sheet.
4. Feel free to pause the DVD player to discuss what you see occurring. However, the first time through the DVD, the flow is important to observe and too many pauses can distract from that. With mutual agreement, feel free to watch the DVD by yourself, always with the dialogue sheet to track what you see occurring on the screen.

How to Get Your Point Across…
Without Puncturing Someone in the Process

    I. *The Outcome*
       A sense of being understood, cared for, accepted
    II. *Strategies*
       For the talker (teacher):

1. Cannot use "you."
2. Be specific and brief.

For the listener (learner):
1. Repress your own feeling and observation.
2. Summarize with same emotional intensity.
3. Summarize without using "I"; use "you" instead.
4. Summarize accurately, even if you disagree.

III. Procedure (for each question)

1. Listener asks question.
2. Talker responds.
3. Listener summarizes.
4. Talker approves or corrects.
5. Listener summarizes.
6. Listener asks next question.

IV. Questions (always asked by listener)

1. "How do you see (view, etc.) this issue (problem, topic, etc.)?"
2. "When this happens, how does it make you feel?"

   LISTENER: Look for hurt, anger, or fear areas.
3. "Can you tell me why you feel this way?"

   TALKER: Usually this question taps into your life history and personal experiences.
4. "What do you need from me when you feel like that?"

   LISTENER: Listen for specific behaviors.

   TALKER: Slow down, think through what you need from listener when this issue arises. Make it a specific behavior. For example: "I need you to start this/stop that … "

V. Change Roles

The talker now asks, "How do you *feel* about what I have just said?" (this is equivalent to question 2 above). Go through the basic questions (2–4) again.

Troubleshooting

1. If you as the talker are feeling "attacked," the listener has assumed your role and is no longer listening.
2. If you as talker are feeling "grilled" or "interrogated," summaries are not being given often enough or at all.
3. If you as a listener are feeling "confused," not enough "feeling" words are being used.
4. Watch out for the talker who says "I feel..." but is using cognition; if you can substitute "I think," then it is probably not a feeling.

5. If you as a listener are feeling "overwhelmed," slow the conversation down; go "down" deeper into the topic instead of "across" the surface of it; limit feelings to those occurring in one issue at a time.

6. When you both are ready to try the process (don't try it when you're both exhausted late at night), sit knee to knee, close enough to touch, and choose roles: *talker* and *listener.* The spouse who naturally talks the most in the marriage should be the first listener; and the talker always chooses the topic. Make sure everything is out of your laps (the listener can hold the dialogue sheet for direction and a Feeling Words list can be on the floor accessible to both of you as needed). Make sure you have at least a half-hour of uninterrupted time available for your first trial.

CAUTION: The first time you begin the dialogue process might be difficult, but don't quit. Most initial failures occur when the *listener* wants to suddenly start talking about how he/she sees an issue, or when the *talker* starts blaming the *listener* by using "you" instead of "I." Remember, *stay in your roles!*

7. The dialogue starts by the *listener* asking the *talker* what he/she would like to talk about. The response: "I would like to talk about how I feel when [issue #1] occurs." (Remember, do not speak "you" here. [That will take some work!] If you have to use the word *you* in this first response, make sure it is not said in a condemning fashion.)

8. The *listener* summarizes the topic to be discussed to the *talker's* satisfaction. If the *listener* doesn't understand the topic or thinks the description is too brief or needs some enhancement, he should ask for that right up front, after the *listener's* first question. Following that enhancement, the *listener* should summarize again until the *talker* is satisfied that the *listener* understands precisely the topic that they are going to talk about. With all this said, give it a try.

CAUTION: Many times a summary is perfect, but it doesn't feel that way to the *talker.* The reason: When the *talker* hears the summary, it often causes a shift in the *talker's* perception. A good summary often refines what was said by the *talker* (just be careful, *listener,* not to plant any of your own ideas into the summary—this by force of habit, often occurs). I often use the illustration of a child's kaleidoscope that, when turned, changes the pattern you see. That is what often happens to the *talker* as they hear what they said come back to them from a little different angle.

9. When the *listener* comes to the question in "What do you need from me when you feel like this?" the *talker* is given permission to use the word "you" for the first time. *You* should be used in terms of "I need you to do this" or "I need you to stop that," etc. Be specific.

CAUTION: The common failure here is to be too vague about what you need. An example of a too-vague statement on the part of the *talker* is, "I just want to be understood." This "need" is so amorphous, so intangible, that it's hard to measure and know when it has been met.

So, *listener*, if you are uncertain of what to do or how to respond, make sure you ask the following question: "What would I have to do for you to feel like...?" (Insert the talker's need being met here; for example, "...I understand you.") A sample reply might be, "I need you to stop reading the paper and give me your full attention." Pin the *talker* down. It doesn't do either of you any good to walk away from a conversation like this, uncertain of how to satisfy your spouse.

---

10. Continue through the process—asking the question, listening, summarizing the answer, then asking the next question—until you have gone all the way through the sequence. At the end, the *talker* needs to ask the *listener* the question at the bottom of the dialogue sheet: "How do you feel about all that I have just said?" Now the *talker* becomes the *listener* and summarizes the feelings that they had in response to the question.

The emphasis here is not so much on the other spouse's perceptions of the topic at hand, but rather on their response to their spouse after being in this process. Usually the spouse feels closer to the *talker*; sometimes a bit surprised; often more hopeful than he felt in a long time; excited about applying what he heard; etc. These are the kinds of feelings that this question is intended to solicit from the *listener*.

11. When finished, at least this first time around, write a brief paragraph about how you felt going through this process. Share your thoughts with your spouse.

_____

_____

_____

_____

The Dialogue

In chapter 2, under "Three Primary Issues," each of you chose three topics for a dialogue, for a total of six dialogues. You will complete number one here, at the end of chapter 6. Then you will do one dialogue to wrap up each chapter until the six are done. Use separate paper, as you did for the first one.

Dialogue number 1   _____

Topic   _____

Talker _____

Note

1. The concept of five love languages in marriage is explored fully in *The Five Love Languages* by Gary Chapman (Chicago: Northfield, 2004).

FEELING WORDS

MAD	SAD	GLAD	AFRAID	CONFUSED	ASHAMED	LONELY
Bothered	Down	At Ease	Uneasy	Curious	Uncomfortable	Out of Place
Ruffled	Blue	Secure	Apprehensive	Uncertain	Awkward	Left Out
Irritated	Somber	Comfortable	Careful	Ambivalent	Clumsy	Unheeded
Displeased	Low	Relaxed	Cautious	Doubtful	Self-Conscious	Lonesome
Annoyed	Glum	Contented	Unsettled	Unsettled	Disconcerted	Disconnected
Steamed	Lonely	Optimistic	Hesitant	Hesitant	Chagrined	Remote
Irked	Disappointed	Satisfied	Tense	Perplexed	Abashed	Invisible
Perturbed	Worn Out	Refreshed	Anxious	Puzzled	Embarrassed	Unwelcome
Frustrated	Melancholy	Stimulated	Nervous	Muddled	Flustered	Cut Off
Angry	Downhearted	Pleased	Edgy	Distracted	Sorry	Excluded
Fed Up	Unhappy	Warm	Distressed	Flustered	Apologetic	Insignificant
Disgusted	Dissatisfied	Snug	Scared	Jumbled	Regretful	Ignored
Indignant	Gloomy	Happy	Frightened	Unfocused	Remorseful	Neglected
Ticked Off	Mournful	Encouraged	Repulsed	Fragmented	Guilty	Separated
Bristling	Grieved	Tickled	Agitated	Dismayed	Disgusted	Removed
Fuming	Depressed	Proud	Shocked	Insecure	Belittled	Detached
Explosive	Lousy	Cheerful	Alarmed	Dazed	Humiliated	Isolated
Enraged	Crushed	Thrilled	Overwhelmed	Bewildered	Violated	Unwanted
Irate	Defeated	Delighted	Frantic	Lost	Dirty	Rejected
Incensed	Dejected	Joyful	Panic Stricken	Stunned	Mortified	Deserted
Burned	Empty	Elated	Horrified	Chaotic	Defiled	Outcast
Burned Up	Wretched	Exhilarated	Petrified	Torn	Degraded	Abandoned
Outraged	Despairing	Overjoyed	Terrified	Baffled	Devastated	Desolate
Furious	Devastated	Ecstatic	Numb	Dumbfounded	Degraded	Forsaken

Each column is marked "A Little" near the top and "A Lot" near the bottom.

Source: Cited in Beverly Hartz, "Pastoral Care and Chaplaincy" class notes, Fall 2000, Talbot Theological Seminary.

7

Family-of-Origin Practices that Predisposed Our Marriage to Infidelity

his is the final project that you and your spouse will do as a part of this workbook. It will help bring closure to this period in your life.

Earlier I told you that you will not be finished with this process until more time has passed. But the basic questions "*How* could you do this to me?" and "*Why* did you do this?" will be answered by this paper you will write together. Much of the content that will be part of this account has already been discussed by you and your spouse in the monologues, homework assignments, and other late-night discussions. But now the two of you will reduce those monologues, assignments, and discussions in an organized fashion. This will pull it all together and add something almost magical to the process. Most couples are delightfully surprised at the outcome of the finished final project.

The Final Project

This final project—a four-chapter account—will take some time. I suggest you try to write only one chapter a week individually. Then, when you have both finished a chapter, share it with each other. After you both complete all four chapters, one spouse should volunteer to merge the papers into a single manuscript that reflects your shared story about this affair.

This paper could be given to a stranger, who upon reading it would say, "I understand fully why this affair happened. It makes all the sense in the world to me." This joint manuscript can be the paper that your adolescent or adult children may read to both protect their future (or current) marriages and to help them understand the process you've been through. This paper is what you can share with other family and friends as the need arises. It especially can be what you would share with couples who will come out of the woodwork asking you for help dealing with their own affair.

The four chapters and their descriptions follow; together they will make up chapters 7–10 of this workbook. (You will, of course, continue to do a dialogue at the end of each chapter as part of your homework.) I suggest that you write the paper on a computer. (It makes it easier to merge both your chapters into a single unit at the end.) If you cannot use a computer but write it by hand, it might be good to attach it to this workbook so that it doesn't get lost—staple it, for example, or use a strong clip.

I have seen this final project run from six to sixty pages. Everyone has a different story, and it is not the length that matters. You might find, though, that you want to add new material to these chapters later in your journey.

Below you will find a brief description of each chapter's content. The remainder of this chapter will be devoted to working on your first chapter of this final paper; subsequent workbook chapters will address the other three assignment chapters.

Chapter 1: Family-of-Origin Practices

The first chapter will discuss family of-origin practices that predisposed the marriage to infidelity. The key word here is *practices*.

What attitudes, beliefs, values, rules, roles, etc., did you bring from your family of origin into your marriage that put it at risk for infidelity? The key phrase to help make the transition from your family of origin to your marriage is "... and as a result, in our marriage ..." This chapter is not just about facts from your family, but rather what you saw, heard, and experienced as a child that you assumed to be the right (and maybe the only) way to run a marriage. These things obviously turned out to cause dysfunctional effects in your family of origin.

If any thoughts come to mind immediately, jot them down in the workspace below.

_____

_____

_____

_____

_____

_____

Chapter 2: Patterns the Spouse and You Developed in the Marriage

The second chapter will explore patterns that the spouse and you developed in the marriage that predisposed it to infidelity. The key word here is *patterns*.

What patterns of interaction did you repeat over and over, to the point they became habitual—and set your marriage on a course to infidelity? These patterns, though painful at times and certainly disappointing, were nevertheless predictable. Each of you knew exactly how to dance this dance. Ironically enough, predictability is usually more attractive to dysfunction than is pain-free living. Strange, but true.

If any thoughts come to mind immediately, jot them down in the workspace below.

_____

_____

_____

_____

_____

_____

Chapter 3: Circumstances that Triggered the Infidelity

The third chapter will discuss circumstances that triggered the infidelity. The key word here is *circumstances*.

This affair did not just happen. There was a cluster of transitions, circumstances, environments, and events that prepared the infidel and initiated this affair. Every infidelity has a different "critical mass" that is necessary for the infidel to stray. Since life is cyclical (we tend to repeat patterns), it is important that you as a couple understand what was involved in the first experience. This chapter will provide some great protection for the future.

If any thoughts come to mind immediately, jot them down in the workspace below.

_____

_____

_____

_____

_____

_____

Chapter 4: Things I Have Learned and Changes I Have Made

The fourth chapter will look at things you have learned and changes you have made. The key word here is *changes*.

This chapter is basically a listing of insights, understandings, triggers, vulnerabilities, etc., that place each of you at risk for someone else's attentions. In your discussions and work up to this point, you have worked out new ways to conduct both your thought life and your behaviors, ways which will greatly decrease the attraction that these things will have on you in the future. By listing the changes you have made with all this information, you are reassuring yourself and especially reassuring your spouse that you will never do this again. We are talking here about changes that really matter—internal awareness, resulting in an external behavioral change.

If any thoughts come to mind immediately, jot them down in the workspace below.

_____

_____

_____

_____

_____

_____

Family-of-Origin Practices

1. Your Parents' Marriage

Each of us brings to the marriage preconceived ideas about how the marriage should work. Most of these ideas are framed in response to our reactions and responses to the marriage we watched as a child. In many cases, even though in reality as young marrieds we were quite uncertain about how a marriage really works, we acted as though we were completely knowledgeable. Who wants to appear "stupid" at one of life's most basic relationships? Besides, where do you go to get trained on how to live in a marriage? And even beyond this, few of us in late adolescence and the early adult years had any clue about what our real, unmet needs were. We just knew that we wanted to get married.

This is not meant to be harsh. All you have to do is look at Hollywood. Celebrities spend their entire lives trying to find the perfect spouse who will meet all their needs. Though divorce is quite painful, do you think that stops them? Of course not! They usually put together a string of marriages that would stagger us "normal people." (Whatever "normal" means!)

So in this chapter we take a thorough look at the only marriage most of us have experienced (before our own), the marriage of our parents.

Below are some writing exercises to help you organize your observations of your parents' marriage. Jot down just enough information to help you recall the thought for inclusion in the appropriate chapter. If you grew up in a single-parent family or a blended family, skip this section and go immediately to the next section. (If you had both parents of origin for five years and/or later had a blended family, complete this section and then the next section as well.)

Patterns I Saw Practiced between My Parents

Displays of Affection	*Communication Patterns*
1. _____	1. _____
2. _____	2. _____
3. _____	3. _____

Husband/Wife Roles	*Power/Control Issues*
1. _____	1. _____
2. _____	2. _____
3. _____	3. _____

Attitudes My Parents Displayed about Sex	*Manipulations/Means of Influence They Used*
1. _____	1. _____
2. _____	2. _____
3. _____	3. _____

Children Issues	*Conflict/Anger between Them: Issues*
1. _____	1. _____
2. _____	2. _____
3. _____	3. _____

Money Patterns	*Conflict/Anger Patterns*
1. _____	1. _____
2. _____	2. _____
3. _____	3. _____

Nurturance/Fun	
1. _____	
2. _____	
3. _____	

2. Blended Family and Single-Parent Family

If you grew up in a blended family or in a single-parent family, complete this section; otherwise, go to the next section. As you consider the blended family or single-parent family you grew up in, do not just concentrate on the facts of your family, but also think in terms of how those facts have impacted your marriage. This might be painful, it might open up some old wounds, and it will probably require you to talk with some siblings or step-siblings about this family dynamic.

It is safe to say that many marriages and subsequent affairs are futile attempts to meet a parental deficit caused by the absence of one of your parents (as a result of their divorce). When a woman doesn't have a biological father present growing up, for example, she often hopes a husband can fill some of her unmet needs. Significantly, if her mother was struggling to survive economically, the mother probably didn't have much time or energy to care for the children emotionally. One of her daughters marries, secretly hoping that her spouse will meet some of those needs. That is why this work is necessary—for the prevention of future infidelity.

How did you handle the following issues common to this family pattern?

1. Loss of parent: _____
_____
_____
_____

2. Loss of friends and neighborhood: _____
_____
_____
_____

3. Loss of grandparents/extended family: _____
_____
_____
_____

4. Adjustment to lower economic status: _____
_____
_____
_____

5. Adjustment to visitation/different family space: _____
_____
_____
_____

6. Adjustment to different family rules/schedules: _____
_____
_____
_____

7. Adjustment to custodial parent dating/remarrying: _____
_____
_____
_____

8. Weekend living in the blended family: _____
_____
_____
_____

9. Connecting to stepparent: _____
_____
_____
_____

10. Connecting to the absent biological parent who has a new spouse: _____
_____
_____
_____

11. Connecting to new space (bedroom, privacy issues): _____
_____
_____
_____

12. Connecting to siblings, step- and half-siblings: _____
_____
_____
_____

3. Unique Family Settings

If your family went through any of the following experiences when you were a child, write about how that situation has impacted your marriage.

1. Death of a family member: _____
_____

2. Chronic illness that impacted parents/family schedule: _____
_____

3. Multiple moves/transfers/parents' poor job history: _____
_____
_____

4. Grandparents living in the home/children living with grandparents: _____

_____

_____

5. Living with individuals other than parents/foster parents/adoption history:

_____

_____

6. Large inheritances, windfalls, financial reversals: _____

_____

_____

Time to Write . . . and Reflect

After conceptualizing this first chapter of the message, it is important that you write it out, as if you were writing a small book about your relationship. Leaving it in the form above is leaving it undone. Writing it out forces you to think more clearly about the impact of it all; it also helps develop insight and understanding—the purpose for doing this exercise in the first place. The blanks above are not intended to represent the chapter's final form, but rather to assist you in organizing your material.

Take several days to write and rewrite the chapter. Once you have finished, answer the following questions prior to sharing the material with your spouse.

What overriding impression do I now have of my family's influence on the infidelity in my marriage?

_____

_____

_____

_____

_____

_____

What new insights did I develop going through this exercise . . .

. . . *about my family of origin and their interactions?*

1. _____

2. _____

3. _____

. . . about the selection of my spouse and the initial purpose of my marriage?

1. _____
2. _____
3. _____

. . . about the development of our marital interactions?

1. _____
2. _____
3. _____

Now exchange chapters with your spouse and read each other's first chapter silently. With permission, mark items that catch your attention using the following legend:

! = significant experience
? = uncertain what this means
+ = good insight
x = I would like to talk some more about this

Afterward, take some time to discuss each other's perceptions, especially those items you marked with a ? or an x. Reflect on your spouse's ideas; begin to fold them into your own thinking. Remember, this eventually will become a joint effort at producing a summary paper.

HOMEWORK

Your Rituals

The strength of a friendship often can be measured in its rituals—those regularly occurring practices that each party anticipates and participates in. Rituals range from the simple (coffee at a certain time of day in a special place or way) to the complex (an annual vacation or tradition).

Believe me, the infidel and the partner either had a set of rituals or were quickly developing them when disclosure took place. All friendships have them. Your dating relationship and early marriage had rituals as well, but sadly, they have been set aside for supposed "utilitarian purposes" (e.g., because of hectic schedules, finances, schooling, lack of energy).

Use the space below to privately recall and record rituals in your personal and joint history. Do not confuse rituals with traditions that are associated with holidays or significant calendar events. Rituals are built around the people involved and the event, not things, such as a certain way to decorate the Christmas tree. They are habits, such as the wife always hugging her girlfriend hello and good-bye, or the husband (and wife) using little pet names for the spouse, or phrases that are unique between the two and that make you feel warm inside.

You began to learn this ritual behavior in childhood friendships and family relationships, then transferred it to your love in adulthood. We will see that in this homework exercise.

What rituals did I develop . . .

... with childhood friends (elementary age)?

1. _____
2. _____
3. _____

4. _____
5. _____
6. _____

... with family members?

1. _____
2. _____
3. _____

4. _____
5. _____
6. _____

... with adolescent friends?

1. _____
2. _____
3. _____

4. _____
5. _____
6. _____

...at college age and dating?

1. _____
2. _____
3. _____

4. _____
5. _____
6. _____

...dating my spouse-to-be?

1. _____
2. _____
3. _____

4. _____
5. _____
6. _____

... early marriage

1. _____   4. _____
2. _____   5. _____
3. _____   6. _____

What rituals were initiated and practiced for a brief period, but now have been abandoned? ("Remember how we used to . . . ?")

1. _____   4. _____
2. _____   5. _____
3. _____   6. _____

What rituals do you currently practice? (These might be difficult to identify because they have become so habitual, but dig—you can find them.)

1. _____   4. _____
2. _____   5. _____
3. _____   6. _____

New rituals I would like to see us develop:

Daily:

1. _____   4. _____
2. _____   5. _____
3. _____   6. _____

Weekly:

1. _____   4. _____
2. _____   5. _____
3. _____   6. _____

Monthly:

1. _____   4. _____
2. _____   5. _____
3. _____   6. _____

Yearly:

1. _____   4. _____
2. _____   5. _____
3. _____   6. _____

Monologue

After writing out the overview of your rituals, share your thoughts with your spouse in a monologue first. Ask for feedback at the end.

Prayer Exercise

Continue to pray daily for your spouse's requests. You should also be more than halfway through with your Compliment Prayer lists. Remember, it will become more difficult the closer you get to the end! Thirty different items is a lot.

Touching Exercises

Do one or two touching exercises this week, whatever is needed to keep the twenty minutes a day, six days a week program going. If you haven't done a head stroking exercise, try that; these can be very meaningful. Don't forget to review the Script Lines Checklist for feelings and thoughts that the touching exercises might generate (this is the list of fifty possible negative reactions to the touching exercises found in chapter 5).

Dialogue

Complete dialogue two, choosing a topic from either your or your spouse's "Three Primary Issues" list developed in chapter 2.

Dialogue number 2 _____

Topic _____

Talker _____

Patterns that Predisposed Our Marriage to Infidelity

The previous chapter focused on what each of you brought into this marriage from your individual families that put it "at risk" for infidelity. This chapter helps you look at the patterns the two of you have developed that set up this marriage for infidelity.

In the beginning of the marriage, the two of you were living together attempting to merge the two styles you were individually familiar with—those of your parents. Gradually over time (generally the first seven years of a marriage), in order to meet the increasing demands of family, the two of you started developing your own patterns. Many of these patterns began with the concept of, "The more you do X, the more I do Y." This is not a conscious thought, but a powerful rationale that produces a self-perpetuating dynamic.

In this chapter, you will explore the ways that you set these patterns in motion. But first, it might be helpful to revisit chapter 3, where you explored your marital style.

Below are several identified categories requiring marital interactions. Complete "Agree…or Disagree?" alone, then discuss each section with your mate; see if he/she agrees with you or not. Keep in mind that the purpose of this exercise is not to become critical or point fingers, but to understand the areas of conflict and again consider your marital style. Be honest. Similarly, the spouse who checks either yes or no should do so honestly, feeling neither defensive nor intimidated in indicating whether he/she agrees. Remember, in the final paper, this material will help you write chapter 2, "Patterns in Our Marriage that Put It at Risk for Infidelity."

Agree... or Disagree?

Sample:

	Spouse in Agreement?	
Money	Yes	No
The more I tried to save money, the more you made fun of me.	○	⊗

....

Money	Yes	No
The more I _____ , the more you _____ .	○	○
The more I _____ , the more you _____ .	○	○
The more I _____ , the more you _____ .	○	○
The more I _____ , the more you _____ .	○	○

Sex		
The more I _____ , the more you _____ .	○	○
The more I _____ , the more you _____ .	○	○
The more I _____ , the more you _____ .	○	○

Fun		
The more I _____ , the more you _____ .	○	○
The more I _____ , the more you _____ .	○	○
The more I _____ , the more you _____ .	○	○

Communication

	Yes	No
The more I _____ ,	○	○
the more you _____ .		
The more I _____ ,	○	○
the more you _____ .		
The more I _____ ,	○	○
the more you _____ .		
The more I _____ ,	○	○
the more you _____ .		

Household Chores

	Yes	No
The more I _____ ,	○	○
the more you _____ .		
The more I _____ ,	○	○
the more you _____ .		
The more I _____ ,	○	○
the more you _____ .		

Children

	Yes	No
The more I _____ ,	○	○
the more you _____ .		
The more I _____ ,	○	○
the more you _____ .		
The more I _____ ,	○	○
the more you _____ .		

In-Laws

	Yes	No
The more I _____ ,	○	○
the more you _____ .		
The more I _____ ,	○	○
the more you _____ .		
The more I _____ ,	○	○
the more you _____ .		

Friends   Yes   No

The more I _____ ,   ◯   ◯

the more you _____ .

The more I _____ ,   ◯   ◯

the more you _____ .

The more I _____ ,   ◯   ◯

the more you _____ .

The more I _____ ,   ◯   ◯

the more you _____ .

Spiritual Practices

The more I _____ ,   ◯   ◯

the more you _____ .

The more I _____ ,   ◯   ◯

the more you _____ .

The more I _____ ,   ◯   ◯

the more you _____ .

Emotions/Intimacy

The more I _____ ,   ◯   ◯

the more you _____ .

The more I _____ ,   ◯   ◯

the more you _____ .

The more I _____ ,   ◯   ◯

the more you _____ .

Use the material from "Agree … or Disagree?"—and the corresponding material your spouse completes—as the springboard for writing chapter 2. Remember, writing out the chapter (rather than leaving it in the above outline form) will cause you to think more clearly about the impact of these areas, and it will help you to develop insight and understanding. Then rewrite the chapter a couple of days later. After writing chapter 2, exchange your copy with your spouse, and mark according to the legend used in chapter 1.

! = significant experience

? = uncertain what this means

+ = good insight

x = I would like to talk some more about this

This will also give you opportunities to clarify and talk further as you get answers to ? and x in the legend. After discussing this chapter, spend some time reviewing each other's homework that was used to organize this chapter (i.e., the exercises above and any other notes you may have). "Teach" your spouse what each area means to you and how it works. Remember, this is not a fight to prove who is right. This is simply your perception of the pattern that the two of you have developed over time in a particular area. Listen closely to each other.

HOMEWORK

Spousal-Selected Monologue

This kind of review provides lots of "fodder" for discussion and for spousal-selected monologues (SSM). Write out three SSM topics from your review of your spouse's workbook preparation for chapters 1 and 2. These are topics about which you would like to hear your spouse elaborate.

Topic

1. _____

2. _____

3. _____

A "Worlds" Monologue

Each marriage has a special universe in which the two spouses live; it's where the individual worlds of the two people orbit around each other. Picture a diagram comprised of two circles: one labeled "his world" and the other "her world." Each spouse has very definite ideas of how those worlds have connected, overlapped, and moved toward (or away from) each other. However, often the *perception* of how the worlds relate varies widely from the spouse's perception.

In each work space below, draw a circle for you and one for your spouse that represents your "universe": your time at work, time at home, time and energy spent in recreation, child-rearing, hobbies, friendships, setting and achieving your goals, etc. Place the two circles in their respective positions (as you see them) relative to each other (e.g., far apart, near to each other, overlapped to a small or large degree) that reflect the pattern of distance or closeness at the time (the season of life) noted in each heading. You can make the circles bigger or smaller to show how the "size" of your world compared to your spouse's world (that is, did one world dominate the other, in your view?). You can also put an arrow within each circle to identify the direction that "world" is going.

Finally, you can add some other descriptors that explain why the circles are so placed. In summary, the closeness or distance of the circles, their size, and the direction they are heading are the three major factors.

A suggestion: Use pencil, because after some interaction on the placement, you might want to revise the circles' positions!

A sample is included: "Ninety Days after the Birth of Your First Child." In its graphic of the two worlds, notice those worlds are overlapping only slightly, reflecting the fatigue and change this couple feels with the addition of a family member. The wife is up a lot at night. She feels worn out when her husband arrives home from work. In turn, the husband now has a "second shift" of household chores and child care. Both find the time they used to have for each other consumed by the child. Their freedom to leave the home, to even go out on a date, is sharply curtailed. Often, the arrival of a baby drains the family income significantly, which takes time to adjust to.

Connecting Two Worlds

Sample:
Ninety Days after the Birth of Your First Child

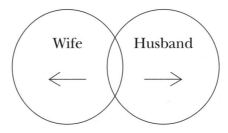

Descriptors: exhausted, focusing just on what I had to do to get by, no time w/ mate; love baby but am borderline miserable about how baby has changed our relationship (no energy even to address that, just worried about it).

Onset of Dating (What Pulled You Together?):
Your worlds:

Descriptors: _____
_____
_____
_____

One Year after Dating Began:
Your worlds:

Descriptors: _____
_____
_____
_____

Newly Married:
Your worlds:

Descriptors: _____
_____
_____
_____

Marriage at the One-Quarter Mark (Based on Number of Years Married before Affair Was Discovered):
Your worlds:

Descriptors: _____
_____
_____
_____

Closest We've Ever Been (What Caused This?):
Your worlds:

Descriptors: _____
_____
_____
_____

Farthest Apart We've Ever Been (What Caused This?):
Your worlds:

Descriptors: _____
_____
_____
_____

Marriage at the Midpoint:
Your worlds:

Descriptors: _____
_____
_____
_____

Marriage at the Three-Quarter Mark:
Your worlds:

Descriptors: _____
_____
_____
_____

Marriage Just Prior to the Affair:
Your worlds:

Descriptors: _____
_____
_____
_____

Marriage Since Disclosure of Infidelity:
Your worlds:

Descriptors: _____
_____
_____
_____

Where I would like to be in terms of closeness/overlap of worlds (How might this be accomplished?):
Your worlds:

Descriptors: _____
_____
_____
_____

Dialogue

Complete dialogue three, choosing a topic from either your or your spouse's "Three Primary Issues" list developed in chapter 2.

Dialogue number 3 _____
Topic _____
Talker _____

9

Circumstances that Triggered the Affair

As stated throughout this workbook, sometime prior to the initiation of the affair, your marital environment had reached the threshold necessary for its occurrence. During this critical-mass stage, the question was not "*Will* an affair happen?" but rather "*When* will it occur—and with whom?"

Often, though, the future infidel is not fully aware of how prepared he/she really is for infidelity; later, in hindsight, the individual begins to put the various pieces together. That is the "bad news." The "good news" is that since life is cyclical, any relationship work you do now, any understanding you gain today, will serve to protect you in the future—from a recurrence in the current marriage or a future one.

This chapter will help you focus on how the environmental conditions, your marital patterns, your internal state of being, and your background all collapsed to a certain moment in time and set the stage for the affair.

Work through the following areas separately in preparation for writing chapter 3 of this final project. Remember, this represents your personal perception—your viewpoint—and it might differ from that of your spouse. So listen closely to each other and explore together in a dialogue the finished chapter 3.

High-Risk Factors

The checklist below contains a cluster of experiences that help identify individuals at risk for infidelity. For now, simply mark each item *yes* or *no* according to your personal history. In the right-hand column are brief definitions of the risk factors.

Yes	No		Definition/Potential Risk
High-Risk Personal Factors			
○	○	Sexual molestation	Childhood seduction, abuse, molestation
○	○	Adolescent promiscuity	Sexually active at fifteen or earlier; more than six partners in the teen years
○	○	Learning disabilities/ADHD	High need for reassurance and nurturance due to emotional pain
High-Risk Family History			
○	○	Family history of infidelity	Up to two generations back/need to know
○	○	Single parent/blended family history	A more vulnerable family history
○	○	Physically abusive/chronic, major conflict	Creates high need for nurturance and reassurance
High-Risk Times			
○	○	Loss — death, health, occupational/career	Look to sex for healing and comforting
○	○	Life changes —pregnancy, school years, teens launching, aging	Affair provides reassurance of youth, virility, attractiveness
○	○	Life transitions — moves, promotions	Loss of usual supports/controls
High-Risk Behavior			
○	○	Opposite sex friendship with private conversations	Always begins to mean more to one party than the other
○	○	Conjoint ministry with opposite sex	A shared heart/passion that doesn't exist in the marriage
○	○	"Soloing" in public places alone	Needy individuals are more frequent and aggressive
○	○	Fantasizing about another	Erodes satisfaction with spouse

The Primary Risk Factors

Now go back to each cluster above and identify which item is the primary risk factor within that cluster. Write about your perception in the lines provided.

High-Risk Personal Factors

Primary Risk Factor(s)   *Why?*

_____   _____

_____   _____

High-Risk Family History

Primary Risk Factor(s)   *Why?*

_____   _____

_____   _____

High-Risk Times

Primary Risk Factor(s)   *Why?*

_____   _____

_____   _____

High-Risk Behavior

Primary Risk Factor(s)   *Why?*

_____   _____

_____   _____

Even though most of this material appears to apply to the infidel, the spouse usually already has some strong feelings and well-developed perceptions about these topics as well. Each of you should fill out the above responses as you view it for the infidel. Use your own perceptions to write chapter 3. I would again suggest that you fall back upon the phrase: "…and as a result of _____, I…" to help with the application of a particular risk factor that set up the affair.

Now write chapter 3. Upon completion of the chapter, discuss how you view the precursors to the infidelity. Don't forget to add additional topics from this chapter to your list of future Spousal-Selected Monologue (SSM) topics.

How do you feel about the information above?

_____

_____

_____

At what point were you aware that infidelity was a possibility?

_____

_____

_____

If you did become aware, what did you try to do about it?

_____

_____

_____

As a spouse, could you sense something happening within the future infidel that you attributed to other "safer" issues?

_____

_____

_____

As the infidel, were you ever aware of initially having to "stuff" a surge of feelings for this future partner prior to any thought of getting involved with the person?

_____

_____

_____

HOMEWORK

About this time most couples need very little direction for the homework exercises. A lot of conversation is going on, hopefully by now not so much about the affair as about the relationships, past and present: how and why this happened to us and what we can do to protect ourselves in the future. These final chapters should encourage that process.

Having said that, the two of you should still be engaged in completing all the exercises (with each of you taking turns to initiate the daily practices).

Spousal-Selected Prayer Request

At this point, you should have been praying for your spouse's requests for almost sixty days (remember the 3 x 5 card in chapter 1?). Furthermore, you should be in the third week of the thirty-day Compliment Prayer exercise (chapter 6). When you have completed this last exercise, exchange notebooks and read how well you are liked, admired, and appreciated! Then, and only then, tackle this next assignment.

Even with all kinds of mixed feelings that you are sure to have, ask your spouse this simple question: "What would you like for me to pray for about myself that would help us in our journey together?"

Give your book to your spouse to write the request in the blanks below. By asking your spouse to give you a request, you are committing to pray for yourself three times daily for the request he/she gives you. (A good time to do this is when you pray for your spouse's three requests.)

My spousal-selected prayer request for you is:

_____

_____

_____

CAUTION: Be careful! You just might receive what you have asked your spouse to pray for! Make sure you are convinced this will be helpful. Do not choose the most difficult life change possible. If your spouse asks you to pray for something that you just cannot do, share that fact. Then promise them that you will pray for God to change your mind and to help you become willing to pray this difficult prayer.

Spousal Prayer

Each of you should still be praying for your spouse's three choices on a daily basis.

Compliment Prayer List

Each of you should be getting pretty close to that magical thirty mark of different characteristics that you appreciate about your spouse. Jointly, you should still be thanking God for a new and different quality in the other spouse's presence on a daily basis. Above, I provided the next level prayer request for those of you who have completed this assignment.

Touching Exercise

Those three nonsexual touching exercises should become a regular part of your daily connection. These are the nurturing touches that build trust. Keep investing in your spouse—and yourself.

Monologues and Spousal-Selected Monologues

One of your options for a daily homework exercise can always be one of these two choices. The twenty-minute time limit makes it safe for both parties. Don't forget the "feedback" option if you are comfortable with it.

Dialogues

This dialogue process will become increasingly important to the full restoration of the marriage. This is the process you use to work through the difficult issues necessary for each of you to stay in this marriage and be happy. This structured talking/listening process will make it safe for you to discuss the most difficult subjects, as long as each of you follow the rules specific to your role.

If you are having difficulty following this procedure, consider looking for some professional help or call one of the organizations listed in the resource pages for referrals to help in your locale. It is possible, given all the corporate and paraprofessional training available today, that you can find a mutually respected friend familiar with these concepts who will hold both of you to the rules. Whatever tack you take, don't let these issues stay unresolved. Each of you may tolerate this condition for a while, but eventually it will come back to undo much of the good that you have accomplished.

Now complete the next dialogue, using the format below.

Dialogue number 4 _____

Topic _____

Talker _____

Review of the Issues

In chapter 2 you each identified three issues that needed to be resolved for you to stay in the marriage and be happy. Reread your listing on page 42. Assuming the three primary issues were serious enough to pull the marriage relationship down to the depths (it was as low as it could go), put a 0 value at the end of each statement. Now, looking at the progress you have made in the past couple of months, assign an improvement score from 1–10 to each (10 is high, an excellent improvement). Draw a slash after the 0 and place the number behind the slash.

After completing this rating, answer the following questions. When finished, share with your spouse.

What were your before-and-after scores on each of these issues? Place the numbers in the spaces below.

Issue One: _____   Before/after score_____

Issue Two:_____   Before/after score_____

Issue Three: _____   Before/after score_____

How do I feel about this improvement? _____

_____

_____

_____

Why? _____

_____

_____

_____

What improvement scores do I think my spouse will choose for my three items?

#1_____   #2_____   #3_____

In most cases, there is still room for improvement. But based on the amount of time since disclosure of the affair and time spent in recovery, most couples are pleasantly surprised at the progress they have made.

10

Things I Have Learned and Changes I Have Made

This chapter is short and pretty straightforward. It could appear redundant if you are not careful, so use it to record information that matches the above title that wouldn't fit anywhere else in your final paper. This is a great spot for insight and self-awareness. It is the perfect area to be self-disclosing.

When writing about changes, be concrete. Don't talk much about what you hope to do—rather, nail down what you are doing now, and why. Look at all the areas of your life: work, play, ministry, family, marriage, God, friends, finances, etc.

Complete the lists below; then write your final chapter. Can you believe that you're almost done?

Things I Have Learned:

About me

1. _____
2. _____
3. _____
4. _____
5. _____

About you

1. _____
2. _____
3. _____

4. _____

5. _____

About us

1. _____

2. _____

3. _____

4. _____

5. _____

Changes I Have Made:

In my personal practices

1. _____

2. _____

3. _____

4. _____

5. _____

Toward you

1. _____

2. _____

3. _____

4. _____

5. _____

In our marriage

1. _____

2. _____

3. _____

4. _____

5. _____

At work

1. _____

2. _____

3. _____

4. _____

5. _____

In ministry

1. _____
2. _____
3. _____
4. _____
5. _____

With God

1. _____
2. _____
3. _____
4. _____
5. _____

In our family

1. _____
2. _____
3. _____
4. _____
5. _____

Toward the opposite sex

1. _____
2. _____
3. _____
4. _____
5. _____

You've completed the fourth chapter of your paper. The final project is done. Amazing, isn't it? In our next and final workbook chapter together, I will provide you with some cautions and some directions you might want to note as you continue in your healing process. At this point, though, most couples just need to stay on course, in process, and put some more time between them and the affair. You have worked hard and have made great progress; you have covered more ground in your marriage than you ever thought existed. You are now ready to restore your great moments, the "Eight Greats" of chapter 6. Have fun and keep on growing.

Some Words to Those Not Continuing On . . .

For those couples who are not planning on staying together, I have a few final words. You have probably sensed that the tenor of the workbook in these final chapters has moved toward the assumption that the couples doing this work will stay married. Fortunately, that is true for most couples who have come this far with this material. Unfortunately, and I am sure with some regret on both spouses' parts, you might not be one of those couples. I do hope you have found this workbook helpful to the two of you. I hope it has helped to bring some closure to this relationship and that you have a more balanced perception of both your spouse and of what went wrong in your marriage. I trust you have been able to work through some of the forgiveness necessary and even rebuilt some of the trust on which the two of you can rely, doing whatever conjoint tasks lie ahead of you (for example, parenting minor children).

I would like to leave you with one final word of caution. Living together as husband and wife for a number of years has changed you both. It will take you awhile to put together a new identity apart from the one you developed while living with your spouse. In adolescence it took you several years to form your first adult identity; and after a traumatic separation such as a death or divorce, it will take you an additional couple of years to redo it. Therefore, I strongly encourage you to not get romantically involved with another individual until you have given yourself an appropriate amount of time to put this new identity together. Most of us in the divorce and grief recovery fields would suggest a minimum of eighteen to twenty-four months.

If you short-circuit this process, either by getting involved with another to help you through the grief, or by marrying someone later on to reassure yourself that you are still attractive, desirable, and wanted, you only postpone the inevitable. Two bad things happen in this bad process: First, you attract the wrong kind of people, and second, when you are finished healing, you will not want that individual in your life any longer.

Therefore, take your time to finish off this identity development still ahead of you. Treat each other with respect and carry out your revised involvement with each other in a mutually satisfying manner (as "business partners," for want of a better term—friendly, but not intimate). Your children will love you for it, and the consequences of this infidelity entering your marriage will be lessened in the generation of your children's marriages.

HOMEWORK

Dialogue

For those couples continuing on in the plan for reconciliation, please complete dialogue number 5, using the form below.

Dialogue number 5 _____

Topic _____

Talker _____

11

Into the Future

Marriages are more alike than they are different.

But even when they go through the same tests, trials, and problems, some marriages "look" better than others. Are there real distinctions? Maybe. But the primary distinction between a good marriage and a bad marriage is this: Those in a good marriage know how and when to refresh and refurbish the marriage relationship, while those in a bad marriage don't have a clue how to do either. Oh, one spouse might say, "We need help," but nothing changes and nothing gets better as they drift apart. So here, in this final chapter, I want to highlight three items: your individual "anniversary reactions," your marital cycles, and your marital satisfaction.

Anniversary Reactions

It is common to have what are called "anniversary reactions," those emotional, usually rocky periods one calendar year later that mark the significant events surrounding the affair's discovery, disclosure, and the demanding work of healing the marriage. The trauma of those calendar dates does diminish over time, and I encourage you to be proactive about those dates' arrival each year. Build a new history on those bad dates. Turn those "hitting bottom" dates into one or more of the "pinnacles" mentioned in the next section.

It is also common to have individual periods of sadness for no apparent reason, not related to the anniversary dates. It can be helpful to try to figure out what is causing the sadness of the moment, but more than likely, it is simply a part of the overall grief process.

Through the years I have worked with couples, many have reported that doing the type of work embodied in this workbook can distract from the actual grieving process. You have been so busy "working" on this marriage that there may not have been adequate time to grieve the loss and trauma of the old marriage. This unexplained sadness is a normal response to this trouble. Do, however, make sure that you and your spouse talk about it. If it is unsettling to your spouse because you are expressing more grief than he or she is (maybe you are just a more sensitive, a more emotional person), then you might need to find a friend or a peer counselor to help you work through these final bits of sadness. Sometimes it feels like it will never end!

It will. I promise.

The next two sections of this final chapter will provide some additional discussion opportunities to draw the two of you together. You'll like them!

Marital Cycles

Every marriage goes through both predictable and idiosyncratic (unique to your marriage) cycles of low/high marital satisfaction levels. Hopefully each of you experience similar satisfaction levels at the same time. The following exercise will help clarify those patterns in your marriage, so do this work individually and then get together with your spouse for a discussion.

As you look back on your shared history, identify the experiences and the causes that created the greatest sense of distance from your spouse and how it was corrected.

	Greatest relational distance	*How it was corrected*
1.	_____	_____
	_____	_____
2.	_____	_____
	_____	_____
3.	_____	_____
	_____	_____

Looking to the future, what do you anticipate to possibly be "seasons of distance" and why?

1. _____
2. _____
3. _____

What do you feel needs to be done to either prevent or lessen the impact of this potential drift apart?

1. _____
2. _____
3. _____

Any additional comments about "cycles of distance"?

1. _____
2. _____
3. _____

Lowering the Risk

Many marriages report satisfaction levels along the following curvilinear pattern.

Marital Satisfaction Levels:

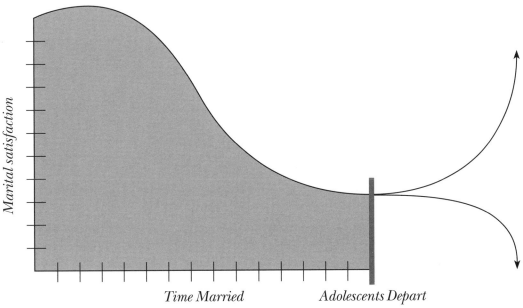

From the chart, it is apparent that marital satisfaction levels reached their lowest point when adolescents are living in the home. Marital satisfaction often begins to drop shortly after the birth of the first child and continues to do so until the children leave home. Good marriages then report an uptick in satisfaction to previous levels—and even above. Other marriages continue to deteriorate until divorce is inevitable. Why?

In the latter case, the purpose which consumed the marriage—child rearing, "the great and noble marriage project"—is over. There is an underlying feeling, an unspoken mutual agreement almost, that might be stated thus: "The kids are raised, we're finished with our task, and this relationship is burned out, used up, and exhausted."

What is a way to prevent this from happening? The good marriage has to develop the skill of nurturing itself by taking periodic "breaks" away from the children, the chores, the routine—time for just the two of you. The purpose is to restore, refresh, and rekindle what brought the two of you together in the first place. This practice helps you create periodic "pinnacles" of high-level satisfaction. These breaks help to:

1. keep hope alive, that when we are done with child rearing, we can still have fun together;
2. build good couple memories during times of very low-level marital satisfaction;
3. alleviate common jealousies that arise from "everyone else having you—and your time and energies—but me."

Most couples are surprised rather quickly about the cost of having children. Money previously available for the marriage now goes to other worthy causes: a washer and dryer, diapers, car repairs, clothes for growing children, etc. To create those "peak" memories in the new era will cost you money. That's something we never have enough of, but remember, you probably didn't have much back in the "good old dating days" either. Still, though, you managed to have fun. With planning, you can do it now, and it might not be as expensive as you fear.

Children not only manage to take most of your money, but they also consume your emotional resources and your time (and that's exactly how it should be). That's why it's better not to have children until they can have you! If you do have children, you still need to take time for yourselves as a couple; you will often have to "steal it" from the children. They might not like it, and they will never truly understand it themselves until they become parents. But remember, better a day or two for you both, on a periodic basis, away from the children than a lifetime of different homes for the kids after divorce!

Creating Peak Memories

These breaks away from the children can become "peak memories" when you practice the following three components:

Childhood Magic—This is the experience of being away from responsibility, not having to go any place at a certain time, able to do what you want, when you want, not having to be a "perfect" model for the children. This is the freedom from bills, chores, and schedules, which is always a part of every affair.

Adolescent Sexuality—This describes those times when you were first married. It was all new; it was passionate, fun, and special. You only thought of each other. This kind of sexuality is spontaneous, chaotic, often unplanned, caught up in the moment, unaware of who else is around, and doesn't care about being "proper" or "quiet"! Remember when you used to hide and make out?

Adult Mobility—This describes the opportunity that every married couple has but rarely takes advantage of. It basically means you choose to seek each other out at unanticipated times. You don't let anyone come before your spouse if that is at all possible. This is the fuel that fires an affair. If you have an hour-and-a-half for lunch, and it takes a half-hour to meet and a half-hour to drive back home, you will still choose to see each other for the thirty minutes that is left. You also choose to travel together at every opportunity. You communicate that I would rather be with you than anybody else on the planet.

After reviewing from above your spouse's love language, your "Eight Greats," your dating relationship, and your early marriage, write out ten activities that you can do as a couple that will create those "peak" memories.

1. _____
2. _____
3. _____
4. _____
5. _____
6. _____
7. _____
8. _____
9. _____
10. _____

Dialogue

Dialogue number 6 _____

Topic _____

Talker _____

Well, we are done. Done with the workbook, that is, but certainly not done with the recovery. As I said in the introduction, the rest of the healing will take time. In that process, I wish you the very best and Godspeed as you continue the journey.

Workbook Homework Schedule

(Page numbers refer to this Workbook)

Session #1
- MSTL (pages 26–28), 3 biographical monologues (pages 25–26),
- Three primary issues (page 42)

Session #2
- F.O.O. (Family of Origin) monologues (pages 35–41)
- Initiate prayer card (page 42)
- Start contribution list (pages 52–55)

Session #3
- Assign chapter 3 – Marital Style (pages 45–55)
- Do family history of infidelity
- Do dialogue #1 in office
- Write forgiveness letter (pages 60–62) at home

Session #4 & Session #5
- Read page 62–63 together at home
- Discuss forgiveness history (pages 57–60)
- Read forgiveness letter in Session #4 or 5
- Both do page 65 monologue at home
- Assign affair forgiveness letter (pages 65–68) to be read at home followed by pages 68–69 (monologue by spouse)

Session #6   • Go over rebuilding trust–chapter 5
                      • Explain & assign touching exercises (pages 77–82)

Session #7   • Eight great moments
                      • Compliment prayer list } Chapter 6 (pages 85–97)
                      • Love languages
                      • Check issues; review and re-do if necessary for the 2nd half

Session #8   Start Final Project Chapter #1: (page 99)
Session #9   Start Final Project Chapter #2: (page 111)
Session #10   Start Final Project Chapter #3: (page 121)
Session #11   Start Final Project Chapter #4: (page 129)

Select Marriage and Recovery Resources

DVD and Internet Resources

Marital Enrichment

1. *The Dialogue DVD Program* This forty-five-minute session features a couple working on one of their primary issues using the dialogue process. This DVD is recommended for steps three and four of the dialogue process (see chapter 6). To order, contact:

   Pastor David Carder
   First Evangelical Free Church
   2801 N. Brea Blvd.
   Fullerton, CA 92835
   dave.carder@evfreefullerton.com
   Cost: $12.00 plus $3.00 shipping and handling; sent priority mail.

2. *GamesforLoving.com* This is an interactive, online series of intimacy building games designed for married couples to play on their laptop. Written by a committed husband and wife team who wanted to enrich their own relationship, the schemes can be adjusted to fit any spouse's comfort level. Lots of these relationship computer games have questionable content, but this is a great communication tool all in the name of closeness and fun.

3. *eHarmonyMarriage.com* Based on a marriage questionnaire, and coupled with their personalized Marriage Profile, each couple is provided video exercises, direction, and tools that will improve their relationship. There is lots of good information about how to put your relationship strengths and styles into practice.

4. *LoversforLife-media.com* Here, in the ultimate Relationship Program developed by Anthony Robbins and Chloe Madanes, are ten steps, done in ten days, to transform your love relationship. There is a CD for each day (or listen online), and a set of follow-up DVDs with an Action Book, designed to help you put into practice what you have been viewing.

5. *MarriageBuilders.com* Very helpful articles on making marriage work after infidelity, but the real action is on the bulletin boards. Navigate to the "discussion forums" and you will find all the options. Language and anger are kept in check by a monitor. Good source for support and lots of encouraging materials.

6. *SmartMarriages.com* This is *the* resource for everything you'll ever need to know about marriages, infidelity, enrichment, skill building, and much, much more. Established by Diane Sollee, former president of the American Association for Marital and Family Therapists, this Web site and the annual conference focus on "take home and do" resources for anyone interested in their own marriage or in helping others.

7. *OCMarriage.org* The home page is called the Orange County Marriage Resource Center, and it lists all the resources being provided in that county during the current calendar month. Options change monthly. Resources are further broken down into five different marriage categories; plus there are other articles and suggestions for new parents, divorcing couples, etc. Though the Web site only lists local offerings, most of these resources are available nationally and even internationally. This Web site is the brainchild of Dennis Stocia, who is committed to lowering the divorce rate in Orange County, California, by half within the next ten years.

Infidelity Recovery

DearPeggy.com A really great site for articles, consultation, lists of therapists, and other support for issues surrounding infidelity recovery. This crusader personally launched the infidelity recovery movement with her book *The Monogamy Myth* and has been involved in the marriage protection effort for almost thirty years.

BeyondAffairs.com Originally the brainchild of Peggy Vaughan, the Berchts continue to provide a nationwide cluster of support groups, seminars, personal phone counseling, and various printed materials. On the home page, you will also find a tab leading to an international listing of the BAN (Beyond Affairs Network) support groups.

Sexual Addiction Recovery

Freedom Begins Here: Introductory DVD Kit Drs. Mark Laaser, Patrick Carnes, and Daniel Amen. Personalized teaching on sexual addiction recovery, with the latest and best information from the co-founders of the original sexual addiction treatment program, Dr. Laaser and Dr. Carnes. This information is coupled with the latest research that Dr. Amen is starting to mine from the world's largest data bank of brain scans. Sexual addiction has biological and biochemical correlates that need to be addressed for successful treatment.

Books

Avoiding the Greener Grass Syndrome. Nancy C. Anderson. Grand Rapids, MI: Kregel Publications, 2004. A brief, easy read with lots of practical suggestions that this couple has implemented to restore and protect their marriage after her affair.

My Husband's Affair Became the Best Thing that Ever Happened to Me. Anne and Brian Bercht. Victoria, British Columbia, Canada; Tadford Publishing, 2004. This is the story of a couple who appeared on the Oprah show in 2005. Besides sharing their personal journey, there are a number of helpful suggestions and resources for your marriage. Anne also offers personal telephone consultation regarding affairs, and together they do marital enrichment seminars across North America.

The Anger Workbook Les Carter, PhD, and Frank Minirth, MD. Nashville, TN: Thomas Nelson Publishers, 1993. This is a very practical, thought-provoking workbook for those struggling with anger in their marriage. Spouses will begin to understand the influence of unmet needs and family of origin influences on their current behavior and, best of all, will be able to choose healthy responses that genuinely reflect their heartfelt desires.

No Stones: Women Redeemed from Sexual Shame. Marnie Ferree. LMFT, Fairfax, VA: Xulon Press, 2002. The only book I recommend for women who are attempting to recover from female sexual addiction. There are very few materials available for the female sex addict, but this is one of them and it is one of the best. Using her own story as a springboard, the author lays out the journey of recovery for women. Besides the book and accompanying workbook, Marnie also provides intensive weekend seminars through a group called Bethesda Workshops.

Not "Just Friends": Rebuilding Trust and Recovering Your Sanity after Infidelity. Shirley Glass, PhD. New York: The Free Press, 2004. This is an easy read and a practical, well-researched book on the topic of emotional and sexual affair recovery. Dr. Glass appeared on numerous radio and TV talk shows right up until her death in 2005.

Redemptive Divorce. Mark Gaither. Nashville, TN: Thomas Nelson, 2008. One of the most positive, practical, directive Christian books for difficult marriages since James Dobson's *Love Must Be Tough.*

Shattered Vows: Hope and Healing for Women Who Have Been Sexually Betrayed. Debbie Laaser. Grand Rapids, MI: Zondervan Publications, 2008. This is *the* book for women and it contains all that Debbie has learned, both in her personal journey of recovery and through helping wives and girlfriends over the last twenty years.

Healing the Wounds of Sexual Addiction Mark Laaser, PhD. Grand Rapids, MI: Zondervan Publications, 2006. Dr. Laaser writes about his personal journey, but his experience with Dr. Patrick Carnes gives him ample credibility. He and his wife, Debbie, continue to offer couple intensives through their clinic in the Minneapolis, MN area.

The Pornography Trap. Mark Laaser, PhD, and Ralph Earle, PhD. Grand Rapids, MI: Zondervan Publications, 2002. Both men come from a faith-based background and have considerable experience working with those trapped by pornography. Their heartfelt compassion, coupled with practical direction, provide a beacon of hope to the sexually addicted.

Unfaithful: Rebuilding Trust after Infidelity. Gary and Mona Shriver. Colorado Springs, CO: Cook Communications, 2005. This is the biographical story of a couple who set about to repair their broken marriage after Gary's disclosure of his affairs. The back and forth conversational style is very helpful to both spouses.

Forgive and Forget: Healing the Hurts We Don't Deserve. Lewis B. Smedes, PhD. New York: Harper Collins, 1984. This is the classic Christian treatment of forgiveness. The fact that it has sold over a half million copies is a testament to its beauty, practicality, simplicity, and sensitivity. Forgiveness doesn't get any better treatment and can't be made any easier to apply.

Getting Past the Affair: A Program to Help You Cope, Heal, and Move On—Together or Apart. Douglas Snyder, PhD, Donald Baucom, PhD, and Kristina Coop Gordon, PhD. New York: The Guilford Press, 2007. Collectively, these three researchers and clinicians have over 100 years of experience in treating difficult marriages. Over the last decade, they have focused their research and clinical efforts on infidelity recovery, and this book contains those efforts to date. Easy to read, built on the latest research, illustrated by their own clinical experiences, this is a top-notch resource.

After the Affair: Healing the Pain and Rebuilding the Trust Where a Partner Has Been Unfaithful. Janis Spring, PhD. New York: Harper Collins, 1996. A practical and compassionate book from the secular market. In my opinion, it is one of the top three books available on infidelity recovery.

How Can I Forgive You? The Courage to Forgive and the Freedom Not To. Janis Spring PhD. New York: Harper Collins, 1999. Though coming from a secular mind-set, Dr. Spring offers some wonderful insight into the necessity and practice of forgiveness after infidelity.

Infidelity: A Practitioner's Guide to Working with Couples in Crisis Paul R. Peluso, New York: Routledge Press, 2007. Though designed for the infidelity clinician and researcher, this book does provide practical, research-based direction for successful therapy outcomes. Clinicians, pastors, and even desperate couples searching for help will find this material encouraging. Though containing all the latest research in this field, it is surprisingly easy to read and quite practical. I especially recommend chapters 4 through 7.

Marital Intensives

Though there are a number of these resources around the country, I like the following two options the best. Most of these programs offer four to eight days of intensive counseling for marriages that need support, healing, love, rest, and major changes within the spousal interactions. The good ones provide quality on-site housing, outstanding meals, wonderful environments, and multiple credentialed therapists. The top programs also have ongoing outcome studies to document their effectiveness. Be aware of discount programs. The quality and costs of these two programs, their outcome studies, and their Christian orientation set the benchmark from which to evaluate other options.

MarbleRetreat.org

Just outside of Aspen, Colorado, this eight-day program was started almost thirty years ago by Dr. and Mrs. Louis McBurney. Marble Retreat has had a long and fruitful history with multiple denominational leaders and only recently has opened up its services to the entire Christian population, both married and single.

NationalMarriage.com

This organization, started by Dr. Gary Smalley (and its accompanying Web site), offers several programs for couples. I prefer the Couples Intensive Program offered in Rome, Georgia. This thirty-hour, four-day program is specifically designed for couples who feel stuck and hopeless in their relationship.

Both of the above programs use the same marital therapy model (developed by the Mayo Clinic), utilize two therapists with the group, and charge almost identical fees. The one major difference is that, given the longer stay, Marble is able to offer each spouse individual therapy as well. Both programs fit well in an infidelity recovery process.

Additional Helpful Books

Adams, Kenneth. *Silently Seduced*. Deerfield Beach, FL: Health Communications, 1991.

Bradshaw, John. *Healing the Shame that Binds You*. Deerfield Beach, FL: Health Communications, 1988.

Brown, Emily. *Patterns of Infidelity and Their Treatment*. New York: Brunner/Mazel, 1991.

Carder, Dave, Earl Henslin, John Townsend, Henry Cloud, and Alice Braward. *Secrets of Your Family Tree: Healing for Adult Children of Dysfunctional Families*. Chicago: Moody, 1991.

Carnes, Patrick. *Out of the Shadows: Understanding Sexual Addiction*. Minneapolis: CompCare, 1985.

Dalbey, Gordon. *Healing the Masculine Soul*. Waco, TX: Word, 1991.

Dobson, James C. *Love Must Be Tough: New Hope for Marriages in Crisis*. Carol Stream, IL: Tyndale House, 2007.

Earle, Ralph, et al. *Lonely All the Time: Recognizing, Understanding and Overcoming Sex Addictions, for Addicts and Co-Dependents*. New York: Pocket Books, 1990.

Love, Patricia. *The Emotional Incest Syndrome.* New York: Bantam, 1990.

Rutter, Peter. *Sex in the Forbidden Zone: When Men in Power—Therapists, Doctors, Clergy, Teachers, and Others—Betray Women's Trust.* Los Angeles: J. P. Tarcher, 1989.

Schneider, Jennifer P. *Back from Betrayal: Surviving His Affairs.* San Francisco: Harper & Row, 1988.

TORN ASUNDER

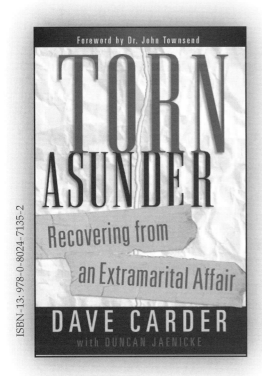

ISBN-13: 978-0-8024-7135-2

Torn Asunder offers couples hope, healing and encouragement in the face of adultery. It helps readers understand extramarital affairs and then offers healing for marriages dealing with this betrayal. This refreshed and updated edition is an excellent resource for pastors, leaders, and lay people.

CLOSE CALLS

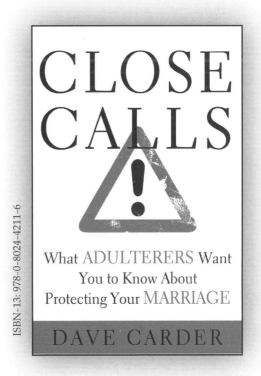

ISBN-13: 978-0-8024-4211-6

Never say never; because just when you think your marriage is safe from adultery is when you may be the most vulnerable. Now, with eye-opening stories, clinical insights, and up-to-date data, Dave Carder reveals what adulterers learned the hard way and want the rest of us to know. *Close Calls* should be on every church leader's and marriage counselor's required reading list.

Ⓜ MOODY
PUBLISHERS.

1-800-678-8812 • MOODYPUBLISHERS.COM

THE 10 COMMANDMENTS
OF MARRIAGE

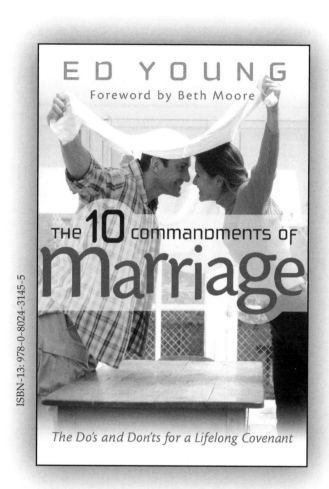

ISBN-13: 978-0-8024-3145-5

In words that are profound, often humorous, but always biblical, Ed Young draws from decades of counseling couples to provide ten commandments for a lifelong marriage that sizzles. God wants your marriage to be nothing short of incredible. And it could all begin with this amazing book.

MOODY
PUBLISHERS.

1-800-678-8812 • MOODYPUBLISHERS.COM